# National Independent Human Rights Institutions for Children

Ursula Kilkelly · Emily Logan

# National Independent Human Rights Institutions for Children

## Protecting and Promoting Children's Rights

palgrave
macmillan

Ursula Kilkelly
School of Law
University College Cork
Cork, Ireland

Emily Logan
Garda Síochána Ombudsman
Commission
Dublin, Ireland

ISBN 978-3-030-80274-5 ISBN 978-3-030-80275-2 (eBook)
https://doi.org/10.1007/978-3-030-80275-2



This Palgrave Macmillan imprint is published by the registered company Springer Nature Switzerland AG
The registered company address is: Gewerbestrasse 11, 6330 Cham, Switzerland

# Preface

The United Nations Convention on the Rights (CRC) was adopted by the General Assembly in 1989 and over thirty years later, the Convention is now well-established as an instrument of international law, with 196 states parties. An important early development, following the establishment of the Committee on the Rights of the Child, was the adoption in 2002 of a General Comment on the role of independent national human rights institutions in the promotion and protection of the rights of the child. This development served to highlight the importance of such institutions at a national level, and to encourage their establishment in states parties. While the Committee highlighted the need to ensure that national institutions for children met the requirements of the Paris Principles, the international standard in the area, the General Comment also made the case for how such bodies should be empowered to protect, promote and fulfil the rights of the child.

National offices of Ombudsman or Commissioners for Children had begun to be established around the world by the time the Committee adopted its General Comment on the subject in 2002 and there has been an interesting diversity in the approaches taken. To date, however, there has been relatively little analysis of their effectiveness in the promotion and protection of children's rights and few opportunities to showcase their important experience of advocating for children's rights at the national level. Ireland established its Ombudsman for Children in 2004, as an independent office with a range of powers to promote and protect children's rights. The purpose of this book therefore is to document the learning from the establishment of this office, highlighting for an international audience some of the methodologies and approaches that have been used to promote and protect children's rights in Ireland. The book presents an original and informed analysis of how a national human rights institution can bring about improvements in the law, policy and practice of children's rights. Reflecting on the span of activity undertaken, primarily in the first ten years of the institution, the book seeks to evaluate the approaches taken by the Ombudsman for Children and reflect on the learning of this experience.

The Irish Ombudsman for Children is an interesting hybrid model of national children's rights institution which combines the 'ombuds' or complaints function with a range of wider powers aligned with the promotion of children's rights. Established against a backdrop of national concern about child abuse and ill-treatment, the Ombudsman for Children has a clear and broad children's rights mandate, which has been used creatively and strategically at times to effect change in a variety of areas. The book is not an analysis of children's rights in Ireland, nor is it a comprehensive account of the role and contribution of the Ombudsman for Children in this regard. What it presents, however, is a specific illustration, through selectively chosen examples and case studies, of how one independent institution for children can influence the national approach to children's rights at a time of great change.

A collaboration of a professor of international children's rights and Ireland's first Ombudsman for Children, the book was co-authored across the professional-academic divide, offering an important means to present enriched analysis from diverse perspectives on a topic of strong, mutual interest. This collaboration aims to inform the academic literature on the reality of leading an independent children's rights institution, while also helping to widen the analytical reference point of those who practice advocacy at the coalface. The authors are both passionate about children's rights and children's rights advocacy and they share an appreciation for the learning achieved through practice and research. Together, they understand the important context of the national experience, while regarding—especially coming from a small country at the edge of Europe—the value of the international perspective. This book is derived from all these factors.

Written during a global pandemic, the conversations about the book, which would normally take place in person and be enriched by wider engagement with our colleagues through casual and formal discussion, took place over Zoom instead. We hope that it prompts fresh conversations across boundaries and jurisdictions about the role and responsibility of national children's rights institutions to advocate for the reform of children's rights.

While this work and any errors it contains are ours, we acknowledge that it is an amalgamation of the learning, wisdom and input of all of those who contributed to the establishment and the development of the Ombudsman for Children's Office over the years. We are grateful to everyone who supported and supports the Ombudsman for Children, who remain committed to ensuring that its capacity to promote, protect and fulfil the rights of the child in Ireland is truly achieved.

Cork, Ireland
Dublin, Ireland
April 2021

Ursula Kilkelly
Emily Logan

# Acknowledgements

**Emily Logan:**
It was my great honour to serve as Ireland's first Ombudsman for Children. At the heart of our office was a small, talented team of like-minded people who were excited at the prospect of making history and who were driven by one aim—improving children's lives. I would like to sincerely acknowledge that team of people and to thank them: Nikki Gallagher, Mánus de Barra, Sophie Magennis, Deirdre O'Shea, Bernard McDonald, Karen McAuley, Aoife Green, Barbara Fowler, Marianne Cassidy, Paraic Walsh. And where would we have been without the support of the wonderful Mary Kearns and Frank Honan?

I would also like to acknowledge others who played a critical role in supporting the Ombudsman for Children's OCO office and more generally for advancing Children's rights in Ireland. Thanks to the Children's Rights Alliance Board who fought for Ireland to have its own Ombudsman for Children, especially the late Ray Dooley who placed children firmly on the political agenda, Justice Catherine McGuinness for her leadership, enduring support and advice, Geoffrey Shannon who was always generous with his time and Fergus Finlay, who always provided wise counsel and was there when things got tough. To the ISPCC and the Directors in Barnardos for keeping us grounded.

I would also like to acknowledge our youth advisory panel, themselves now adults and leaders and to extend gratitude for their guidance and support to the followinginternational children's rights advocates: Thomas

Hammarberg, Maud de Boer-Buquicchio and Marta Santos Pais to name a few. Thanks also to the many Commissioners, Ombudsmen and advocates for children throughout the globe who dedicate their lives to the advancement of children's rights.

Ursula Kilkelly managed to challenge, motivate me and sometimes frighten me in this unique role. I would highly recommend that every newly appointed Ombudsman for Children find themselves a colleague who can do the same!

**Ursula Kilkelly:**

It was my pleasure to work closely with Emily and her colleagues during her term as Ireland's Ombudsman for Children and to see the office go from strength to strength as a model of its kind internationally. I am so pleased to have been able to document some of the lessons from this process and want to thank my co-author Emily for her vision, collegiality and the motivation to get the job done!

Completing this monograph would not have been possible, especially during a global pandemic, without the support of many people—to Josie Taylor at Palgrave for her enthusiasm and guidance, to my colleagues at University College Cork for their flexibility and support and my friends in the global children's rights community for their constant inspiration. A particular thank you to my research assistant Laura Lanigan and also Rose Wallace.

This book is for children's rights advocates everywhere!

# Contents


**1 Introduction** 1

*1.1 Introduction* 2

*1.2 International Standards on National Human Rights Institutions for Children* 3

*1.3 The Emergence of National Human Rights Institutions for Children* 5

*1.4 Ombudsman for Children in Ireland* 7

*1.5 Methodology* 9

*1.6 Structure of the Book* 10

*1.7 Conclusion* 10

*References* 11

**2 National Human Rights Institutions for Children—The International Experience** 13

*2.1 Introduction* 14

*2.2 International Standards on National Human Rights Institutions* 14

*2.3 CRC Standards on Independent Human Rights Institutions for Children* 16

*2.4 Strengths and Weaknesses of NHRIs for Children* 18

*2.5 Conclusion* 26

*References* 27

**3 The Irish Model—The Ombudsman for Children** 29
*3.1 Introduction* 30
*3.2 Background to the Establishment of the Ombudsman for Children* 30
*3.2.1 Ireland's History of Child Abuse* 30
*3.2.2 Advocacy, Research and the Role of Civil Society* 31
*3.2.3 The Role of the UN Committee on the Rights of the Child* 33
*3.2.4 Further Influences on the Ombudsman for Children* 34
*3.3 Ombudsman for Children Act 2002* 34
*3.3.1 Compatibility with International Standards* 37
*3.4 Conclusion* 40
*References* 41

**4 Raising Awareness** 45
*4.1 Introduction* 46
*4.2 Powers to Promote Children's Rights* 47
*4.3 Participation of Children* 49
*4.3.1 The Participation Lab* 50
*4.4 The 'Big Ballot'* 51
*4.4.1 Phase 1: The Academic Research* 52
*4.4.2 Phase 2: Testing the Findings of the Academic Research with Children* 53
*4.4.3 Phase 3: The Vote* 54
*4.4.4 Reflections on the Big Ballot* 58
*4.5 Conclusion* 59
*References* 60

**5 Advising Government** 65
*5.1 Introduction* 66
*5.2 Accountability to Parliament* 68
*5.3 Guidance and Advice to Government* 71
*5.4 Constitutional Reform* 77
*5.5 Conclusion* 81
*References* 82

**6 Complaints and Investigations** 85
*6.1 Introduction* 86
*6.2 The Powers of the Ombudsman for Children* 87

*6.3 The Ombudsman for Children's Approach to Complaints* 88
*6.4 Substance of Complaints Before the Ombudsman for Children* 95
*6.5 Improving Administrative Practice Among Public Bodies* 97
*6.6 Conclusion* 99
*References* 100

**7 Children in Prison** 103
*7.1 Introduction* 104
*7.2 St. Patrick's Institution and the Background to the Project* 105
*7.3 The Ombudsman for Children's Project* 107
*7.3.1 Beginning the Project, Building Trust* 108
*7.3.2 Approach to the Participation of the Children and Young People* 108
*7.4 The Findings of the Consultation* 109
*7.4.1 Committal, Orientation and Sentence Planning* 109
*7.4.2 Separation from Adults* 110
*7.4.3 Accommodation* 111
*7.4.4 Health* 112
*7.4.5 Education, Training and Recreation* 112
*7.4.6 Contact with Family and Community* 113
*7.4.7 Safety, Protection and Disciplinary Measures* 114
*7.4.8 Complaints and Inspections* 114
*7.5 Reaction and Response* 116
*7.6 Engaging International Support* 117
*7.7 Conclusion* 118
*References* 120

**8 Separated Children Seeking International Protection** 123
*8.1 Introduction* 124
*8.2 Separated Children in Ireland* 125
*8.3 The Ombudsman for Children's Project* 127
*8.4 Building the Case for Reform* 129
*8.4.1 Legislative Reform* 129
*8.4.2 Article 2 Non-Discrimination* 130
*8.4.3 Asylum Process* 130

8.4.4 Education 130
8.4.5 *Absence of an Independent Guardian/Adviser* 131
8.4.6 *Complaints Mechanisms* 131
8.4.7 *Aftercare and Protection* 132
8.4.8 *Out of Hours Support* 132
8.5 *Creative Approaches to Chronicling the Children's Experience* 132
8.5.1 *Dublin—Your City, Our City* 132
8.5.2 *'All I Have to Say'* 133
8.5.3 *Creative Art and Photography* 133
8.6 *Conclusion* 134
*References* 135

**9 Conclusions** 139
9.1 *Introduction* 139
9.2 *Origins of the Institution and the Legislation* 140
9.3 *Exercising the Ombudsman's Powers* 142
9.4 *Reviewing for the Future* 143

**Index** 145

# About the Authors

**Professor Ursula Kilkelly** is an international children's rights scholar. Based at the School of Law, University College Cork, Ursula has published and researched across all areas of children's rights—with a focus on children's rights implementation for over 20 years. She is the author of several monographs and edited collections in the area of children's rights with nearly 100 publications on legal implementation of children's rights.

**Emily Logan** has sixteen years of experience leading two national human rights institutions; as Ireland's first Ombudsman for Children and subsequently as Chief Commissioner of the Irish Human Rights and Equality Commission. She is an Adjunct Full Professor at University College Dublin and Adjunct Professor (Human Rights Practice) at the Irish Centre for Human Rights, National University of Ireland, Galway.

# Abbreviations

| | |
|---|---|
| BINOCC | British and Irish Network of Ombudsman and Children's Commissioners |
| CAT | Committee Against Torture |
| CPT | European Committee for the Prevention of Torture and Inhuman or Degrading Treatment or Punishment |
| CRC | United Nations Convention on the Rights of the Child |
| CRC Committee | United Nations Committee on the Rights of the Child |
| ENOC | European Network of Ombudspersons for Children |
| GANHRI | Global Alliance of National Human Rights Institutions |
| GSOC | Garda Síochána Ombudsman Commission |
| HSE | Health Service Executive |
| NHRIs | National Human Rights Institutions |
| OCO | Ombudsman for Children/Ombudsman for Children's Office |
| SCSA | Separated Children Seeking Asylum service |
| UN | United Nations |
| UNHCR | United Nations High Commissioner for Refugees |

CHAPTER 1

# Introduction

**Abstract** The United Nations adopted the Convention on the Rights of the Child in 1989, setting out in international law the rights to which children are entitled and the duties on states parties to protect, promote and fulfil those rights. The Committee on the Rights of the Child, the body that monitors the Convention's implementation, adopted a General Comment on the role of national human rights institutions for children to promote and protect children's rights at a national level and the number and type of such institutions has continued to grow globally. Ireland established its Ombudsman for Children in 2004, combining a complaints function with a broader mandate to promote children's rights. The aim of this book is to analyse how the Irish model meets the international standards in order to contribute to the understanding about how best to ensure such organisations promote and protect children's rights at a national level. It considers in separate chapters the different powers of the Ombudsman for Children, namely promoting awareness, providing government advice and considering complaints. Two case studies illustrate creative approaches to children's rights concerning children in prison and separated children seeking international protection. The book ends with some conclusions and reflections.



U. Kilkelly and E. Logan, *National Independent Human Rights Institutions for Children*,
https://doi.org/10.1007/978-3-030-80275-2_1

**Keywords** National Human Rights Institutions (NHRIs) · Ombudsman for Children · Children's rights · Convention on the Rights of the Child · Implementation

## 1.1 Introduction

Over thirty years ago, the United Nations adopted the Convention on the Rights of the Child (CRC, 1989), the first internationally binding treaty on children's rights and the Convention has now been ratified by all states parties but the United States. The Committee on the Rights of the Child, the body established under the Convention to monitor its implementation, reviews the progress of state parties to the Convention, documenting concerns and progress and making recommendations for improvements as part of the reporting process. The Committee has published 25 General Comments, addressing the Convention's application in specific areas and settings and highlighting the duties on states parties to protect the rights of particularly vulnerable children. General Comment No. 2 was dedicated to independent national human rights institutions for children (CRC Committee, 2002) prescribing the elements that were key to ensuring that the potential of such institutions to advance implementation of the Convention was maximised. This General Comment followed on from a UNICEF INNOCENTI Digest, published in 2001, which noted the importance of national institutions for children to the implementation of children's rights, while acknowledging the increased, but not yet universal, support for such institutions (Lansdown, 2001, p. 1).

Having ratified the Convention in 1992, Ireland enacted legislation to establish its Ombudsman for Children's Office ten years later, in 2002, coinciding with the publication of the Committee's General Comment and the increased global support for national human rights institutions for children. The Irish model is a hybrid institution, with both a complaint ('ombuds') function and a wider mandate to promote children's rights through providing advice to government and raising awareness. In its first decade, in particular, the Office was both creative and effective in fulfilling its mandate, bringing about change in law and policy, improving children's treatment and increasing awareness about their rights. For these reasons, it makes an important case study of how international standards regarding national institutions for children can be used to promote and protect children's rights at a national level. This is the aim of this book and it is the goal of this chapter to introduce the book's themes and to explain our approach.

## 1.2 International Standards on National Human Rights Institutions for Children

Article 4 of the CRC obliges state parties to undertake all appropriate legislative, administrative and other measures for the implementation of the rights recognised in the Convention. According to the Committee on the Rights of the Child (the Committee), the establishment of a national human rights institution for children falls within the commitment made by state parties when they ratify the Convention to take measures to ensure its implementation (CRC Committee, 2003). From an early point, the Committee sought information from states parties during the reporting process on developments to establish 'an independent body to promote and protect the rights of the child, such as an Ombudsman or Commissioner' (CRC Committee, 1996, p. 5) and it has routinely raised the matter of the existence, standing and resourcing of such bodies during the periodic dialogue since (Sedletzki, 2012, p. 7). In 2002, the Committee published guidance in the form of a General Comment on the establishment of independent national human rights institutions for the promotion and protection of children's rights (CRC Committee, 2002), in light of the important role played by such institutions in the implementation of the Convention. It reiterated this recommendation to states parties to establish a national human rights institution for children in its 2003 General Comment on general measures of implementation, where it noted that national human rights institutions for children can act as a complementary mechanism to effective government structures in Convention implementation (CRC Committee, 2003). According to the Committee, national human rights institutions for children should comply with the UN Principles relating to the status of national institutions, adopted following a process of international dialogue on the concept of a national human rights institution (UN General Assembly, 1993). Known as the Paris Principles, these are a set of minimum standards on the establishment, competence, independence and quasi-judicial activities of national human rights institutions (NHRIs) which represent the standard bearer for all NHRIs, including those focused on children's rights. The Principles require that human rights institutions are vested with competence to protect human rights, the responsibility to promote harmonisation of legislation with human rights instruments and an ability to publish independent opinions and reports, including submissions to UN bodies and to promote, teach and publicise human rights. According to Lansdown, these features are equally applicable to independent national human rights institutions for children although she notes that 'the different legal status of children, and the need to take account of their best interests, evolving capacities, and right to express views and have them taken seriously, does require an additional degree of adaptation in the design and orientation of the institutions serving them' (2020, pp. 498–499).

Internationally, the UN now reports 122 national human rights institutions across the four regions of Asia and the Pacific, Africa, Europe and the Americas and there is renewed interest globally in such institutions, following agreement of the Sustainable Development Goals (UN, 2015). One of the indicators for the delivery of Goal Sixteen on Peace, Justice and Strong Institutions includes the existence of independent national human rights institutions in compliance with the Paris Principles. If anything, then, the prevalence of NHRIs is set to further increase over the next decade, in pursuit of the 2030 Agenda for Sustainable Development. Peer practice of national human rights institutions has also continued to evolve since the adoption of the Paris Principles, with the emergence of the Global Alliance of NHRIs (GANHRI, https://ganhri.org/) in 1993, supported by the Office of the High Commissioner for Human Rights to provide accreditation to such institutions.

However, as Lansdown (2020) notes, there are clear differences between national human rights institutions, established and developed in line with the Paris Principles and the standards of the Global Alliance of NHRI's (GANHRI), and the institutions which are focused exclusively on the promotion and protection of children's rights. Although national independent human rights institutions for children are not necessarily 'national human rights institutions' as understood in the context of the GANHRI accreditation system, they nonetheless share the goal of universal human rights protection. At the same time, building on the Paris Principles, the Committee's General Comment No. 2 introduced additional standards for national institutions for children requiring that they operate in line with the Convention's general principles, notably article 2 (non-discrimination), article 3 (best interests of the child) and article 12 (the child's right to be heard), ensuring that such institutions advocate for the implementation of the Convention, while also operating in line with children's rights principles.

## 1.3 The Emergence of National Human Rights Institutions for Children

Within their own terms, national human rights institutions for children are diverse and take many different forms with varying powers, remit, resourcing and standing (Thomas et al., 2011). Some, like ombuds offices, have complaints functions and offer remedies for the breaches of children's rights; others, such as National Commissions and Commissioners for Children, reflect a more proactive range of activities associated with the promotion and protection of children's rights. In one form or another, all such institutions engage in a range of monitoring and auditing functions that seek to hold state authorities to account for the implementation of the Convention, advancing the realisation of children's rights through dialogue, research, public engagement and education. It is this range of monitoring, protecting and promoting children's rights that arguably defines such institutions, making them such vital instruments for Convention implementation.

According to UNICEF (Sedletzki, 2012, p. 5), despite the variety of national human rights institutions for children,

> their ability to effect change results from their combination of independence and 'soft power': the capacity to report, to convene, to mediate and to influence lawmakers, government bodies, public institutions and public opinion. Indeed, it is the ability to influence those with direct responsibility for policy and practice that distinguishes an effective institution.

Despite this diversity and distinctiveness, and notwithstanding their focus on children as a specific group of rights holders, the experiences of national human rights institutions for children are transferable to other more general bodies. This transferability has been recognised most recently by the UN through the development of its national human rights institutions' toolkit and child rights approach (UNICEF, 2018). Studying the operation and impact of such children's rights institutions has thus great potential to enrich the peer experience of more general human rights institutions everywhere.

Since the establishment of the first ombudsman for children in Norway in 1981 (Flekkoy, 1991), the number of independent human rights institutions for children has grown (Lansdown, 2001), in line with increasing state ratification of the Convention on the Rights of the Child (Sedletzki,

2012, p. 5). In 2012, UNICEF estimated that there were over 200 national human rights institutions for children in over 70 countries (Sedletzki, 2012, p. 4). These institutions have also organised regionally, with for instance, forty-three institutions across Council of Europe member states (European Network of Ombudspersons for Children, http://enoc.eu/).

Although the Norwegian model was highly influential in the early years, as Northern Europe led the way in the establishment of such offices in countries with strong human rights and governance traditions, 'democratization in Latin America and the recognition of children as subjects of rights in law and policy paved the way for the creation of children's offices within public defender's institutions' there (Sedletzki, 2012, p. 8). The path to the creation of each institution, and the form it has taken, has to some extent been unique. In the mid-2000s, for instance, countries in Africa and Asia established such offices as part of efforts to comply with international human rights standards for children and in common law countries, like Australia and New Zealand, approaches tended to focus on child protection, with a particular emphasis on vulnerable or marginalised children (Sedletzki, 2012, p. 8). For instance, the protection of children from violence has been noted as a 'catalyst' for the establishment of independent human rights institutions in the African region (Sloth-Nielsen, 2020, p. 289).

Internationally, the human rights role has evolved into an integral part of many ombudsman institutions in what is described as the '"new face" of the ombudsman' (Ayeni, 2014, p. 499). The ombudsman model is now common in Eastern Europe, Central and South America and in the Commonwealth of Independent States (Ayeni, 2014). The newer model of dedicated or specialized institutions for the protection of children's rights includes children's ombudsmen, children's commissioners and children's advocates which now exist in many countries throughout Europe and Latin America, in Australia and Canada (Ayeni, 2014). Although Africa currently has 43 NHRIs, few as yet have 'children's desks' or commissioners although Mauritius notably has had a dedicated ombuds for children since 2003 (Sloth-Nielsen, 2020, p. 293). Even still, it seems relatively rare for countries, like Ireland, to have a hybrid model, with a single institution promoting and monitoring children's rights and investigating maladministration.

## 1.4 Ombudsman for Children in Ireland

In Ireland, the Ombudsman for Children Act 2002 came into force in 2004. The establishment of the office in legislation is compliant with the international standards and both its independence and its range of powers reflect a consistency with the Paris Principles and the Committee's General Comment No. 2 (CRC Committee, 2002). In particular, the Ombudsman is appointed by the Head of State, the President of Ireland, and it is accountable to the Oireachtas (the parliament) with a wide-ranging mandate and powers to promote and protect children's rights. The founding legislation provides for a complaint and investigation function and this is combined with the authority to guide and advise government on draft and operational legislation. The Ombudsman also has a number of powers relating to the promotion of children's rights.

Of most significance in the Irish experience is the way in which the range of powers given to the Ombudsman for Children have been combined in practice. The investigation function, the cornerstone of the institution, has allowed the Ombudsman to uncover the ill-treatment of children: in health and child protection services, in schools and in areas like housing, whereas engaging politically has enabled the institution to advise Government systematically on the compatibility of proposed and draft law and policy with the Convention. Outside of the investigatory remit, the Ombudsman for Children has used discretionary or soft powers of research and inquiry, undertaking strategic initiatives to consult with children for instance, to raise awareness of their rights and to advance reform. Using the Ombudsman's powers creatively has helped to shine a light on children's rights issues that were previously invisible and amplifying their voices has allowed their views and perspectives to be brought into the public domain. As increasing numbers of individual complaints were resolved, the approach became more systemic in focus and it is the targeted use of power, in partnership with children, that has borne most fruit from a children's rights perspective.

Experience indicates that the central tenet of institutional independence was key to the credibility and legitimacy of the Ombudsman for Children institution as it became established. Critical too was the principle that the Office would function in line with the Committee's General Comment No. 2, encapsulating children's voice and best interests into its approach. Independence in status and in operation has helped to shield the institution from political interference, as its credibility—including by ensuring children were centre stage—enabled it to gather public profile and support, and an integrity that is vital to its mission.

Notwithstanding the importance of the national context, national human rights institutions must engage as international actors if they are to leverage international children's rights standards to maximum effect. The dynamic between domestic and international actors is a valuable asset not least because when domestic actors meet resistance nationally, they can turn to international actors for endorsement. This has been a particularly effective strategy in Ireland, a country that cares deeply about its international reputation and place in the world and this approach has enabled the Ombudsman for Children to take on a position of leadership internationally, including through the European Network of Ombudspersons for Children, a large network of 40 independent children's rights institutions across the Council of Europe. During the Irish chair of ENOC, for instance, the Ombudsman for Children established a secretariat and secured ongoing support from the Council of Europe and from the European Commission that endures to this day.

It is evident therefore that in Ireland the Ombudsman for Children has played an influential role in the promotion and protection of children's rights, using its diverse powers to maximum effect to hold government to account on the implementation of the Convention on the Rights of the Child in creative and persuasive ways. At the same time, it has been met with barriers and challenges—both in its operation and in the protection of children's rights—that have curtailed its full impact in some key areas (Kilkelly, 2007). For instance, societal and cultural barriers to the full acceptance of children's rights played out in the political system during the campaign to amend the Irish Constitution in 2012. At other times too, initiatives and proposals for reform were met with resistance. In a process of constructive engagement with academia and civil society, and a commitment to evaluation that supported continuous learning, what has been key to the Ombudsman for Children has been the organisation's ability to adapt and evolve, adhering closely to the guiding principles of children's rights including a commitment to the ultimate goal of their universal promotion and protection.

## 1.5 Methodology

The purpose of this book is to document the learning of the first decade of the Irish Ombudsman for Children, highlighting for an international audience the methodologies that can be used to promote and protect children's rights at a national level. Co-authored by a children's rights professor and Ireland's first Ombudsman for Children, the book presents an original analysis, across the practice-academic divide, of how a national human rights institution can advocate for the rights of children. The book does not propose to analyse comprehensively the multiple achievements of the Ombudsman for Children in Ireland. Nor is it intended as a study of children's rights in Ireland, which has been a very joint effort, brought about in a sustained and careful way by an active and expert civil society and academic community. Instead, this book aims to show case, through the use of selective, illustrative case studies, how the powers of a national human rights institution for children can be put to strategic use. The book aims to present some of the lessons of national children's rights advocacy acquired through the experience of the Ombudsman for Children, in the hope that they will inspire and equip national human rights institutions everywhere to better advance children's rights. To aid the transfer of the learning, the book uses the international benchmarks in the Committee's General Comment No. 2 and the Paris Principles in evaluating the operation of the institution. In highlighting its successes, it seeks to also take a critical stance, noting for instance where reform did not materialise or where other approaches might have achieved better outcomes.

While the value of the Irish experience is in the integrated approach, each chapter here stands alone as an individual case study so that its learning can be extracted, examined and replicated. This approach seeks to maximise the value of the book to the international community reflective of the diversity of NHRI models that exist. The emphasis on the mechanisms of soft power illustrates that they can be as important as the power to investigate complaints. Overall, although it presents just a snapshot of the broad range of activity undertaken by the Ombudsman for Children since its establishment in 2004, its focus is on what can be achieved regardless of the size or form of the national children's rights institution.

## 1.6 Structure of the Book

The book is presented in three sections. This introduction is followed by two further introductory chapters. Chapter 2 sets out the international experience of independent national human rights institutions for children, while Chapter 3 goes on to introduce the Irish model of Ombudsman for Children. There then follow three chapters that document and critique three distinct functions of the Ombudsman's Office, namely Chapter 4 which addresses the duty to raise awareness of children's rights, Chapter 5, which considers the Ombudsman's advisory role to Government and Chapter 6, which details the complaint and investigation function. All three chapters will document how these functions have been developed and delivered and the progress they have made in protecting and promoting the rights of the child.

There are then two impact case studies—the first, Chapter 7, addresses the work of the Ombudsman to bring an end to the use of adult prison for children and the second, Chapter 8 considers the role of the Ombudsman in improving the rights of separated children in Ireland. Chapter 9, in conclusion, brings together all the learning and offers some reflections from the perspective of one national human rights institution for children on what has been instrumental in advancing children's rights.

## 1.7 Conclusion

Against the backdrop of state responsibility to implement the Convention on the Rights of the Child and the increasing recourse to national human rights institutions for children, this book provides an important snapshot of the impact that one such institution—the Ombudsman for Children—can have on law, policy and practice from a children's rights perspective. It demonstrates how legislative authority can be maximised and highlights how both creativity and a rights basis are crucial to maximising the potential of such institutions to protect and promote children's rights. Although an Irish case study, the book takes account of the multitude of models that exist around the world and by situating the learning in an international context it seeks to ensure that this experience is placed at the disposal of similar organisations worldwide.

## References


Ayeni, V. O. (2014). Ombudsmen as human rights institutions. *Journal of Human Rights, 13*(4), 498–511.

European Network of Ombudspersons for Children (ENOC). http://enoc.eu/. Accessed 31 Mar 2021.

Flekkoy, M. G. (1991). *A voice for children: Speaking out as their ombudsman*. UNICEF.

Global Alliance of National Human Rights Institutions (GANHRI). https://ganhri.org/. Accessed 8 Apr 2021.

Kilkelly, U. (2007). *Barriers to the realisation of children's rights in Ireland*. Ombudsman for Children's Office.

Lansdown, G. (2001). *Independent institutions: Protecting children's rights* (Innocenti Digest No. 8). Florence, Italy: UNICEF.

Lansdown, G. (2020). National human rights institutions for children. In J. Todres & S. King (Eds.), *The Oxford handbook of children's rights law* (pp. 495–512). Oxford University Press.

Ombudsman for Children Act 2002.

Sedletzki, V. (2012). *Championing children's rights: A global study of independent human rights institutions for children—Summary report*. Innocenti Publications.

Sloth-Nielsen, J. (2020). The role of national human rights institutions in enhancing the impact of children's rights reporting in Africa. In R. Miamingi (Ed.), *State party reporting and the realisation of children's rights in Africa* (pp. 283–306). Pretoria University Law Press.

Thomas, N., Hanson, K., & Gran, B. (2011). An independent voice for children's rights in Europe? The role of independent children's rights institutions in the EU. *The International Journal of Children's Rights, 19*(3), 429–449.

UN Convention on the Rights of the Child (CRC). (1989).

UN Committee on the Rights of the Child. (1996, November 20). *General guidelines regarding the form and contents of periodic reports to be submitted by States parties under article 44, paragraph 1(b), of the convention*. CRC/C/58.

UN Committee on the Rights of the Child. (2002, November 15). *General Comment No. 2 (2002): The role of independent national human rights institutions in the promotion and protection of the rights of the child*. CRC/GC/2002/2.

UN Committee on the Rights of the Child. (2003, November 27). *General Comment No. 5 (2003): General measures of implementation of the Convention on the Rights of the Child*. CRC/GC/2003/5.

UN General Assembly. (1993). *Principles relating to the status of national institutions (Paris Principles)*. UN Doc. A/RES/48/134.

United Nations. (2015). *Transforming our world: The 2030 agenda for sustainable development*. UN Doc A/RES/70/1.

UNICEF. (2018). *National human rights institutions [NHRI's] series: Tools to support child-friendly practices*. Presentation of the Tool Kit and Child Rights Approach. Available at: https://nhri.ohchr.org/EN/Themes/RightsChild/Documents/Tools%20to%20support%20child-friendly%20practices%20-%20Introduction%20and%20the%20Child%20Rights%20Approach.pdf. Accessed 31 Mar 2021.

CHAPTER 2

# National Human Rights Institutions for Children—The International Experience

**Abstract** This chapter introduces the concept of national human rights institutions for children to provide the international and theoretical context for the analysis of the Irish Ombudsman for Children that follows. It outlines the relevant international standards, including the Paris Principles on NHRIs, as well as the Committee on the Rights of the Child's General Comment No. 2 on the role of independent national human rights institutions in the promotion and protection of children's rights. The chapter makes the case for a distinct form of NHRI for the protection and promotion of children's rights and considers the emergence of such institutions around the world, considering their diverse form and approach. The chapter explains the unique role played by the national children's rights institution as a distinct body, with key lessons as to the features of such bodies that are instrumental for effective promotion and protection of children's rights at a national level.

**Keywords** National Human Rights Institutions (NHRIs) · Paris Principles · CRC General Comment No 2 · Children's rights promotion · Independence · Complaints


U. Kilkelly and E. Logan, *National Independent Human Rights Institutions for Children*,
https://doi.org/10.1007/978-3-030-80275-2_2

## 2.1 Introduction

The UN Convention on the Rights of the Child (CRC, 1989) placed children's rights firmly on the international stage, while Article 4 of the Convention requires the implementation of such rights at the national level. One of the early steps taken by the UN Committee on the Rights of the Child (the CRC Committee) was the adoption of a General Comment on the role of independent national human rights institutions in the promotion and protection of children's rights (CRC Committee, 2002). Building on the Paris Principles on national human rights institutions (NHRIs) (UN General Assembly, 1993), the General Comment identified how such institutions were to function in order to further implementation of the CRC. National children's rights institutions vary in form and approach, existing as ombudspersons, commissioners for children or as children's desks or commissions within wider national human rights bodies. Their growth in popularity and standing has been supported by the monitoring work of the CRC Committee and other international bodies like UNICEF in recognition of the impact that they can have in the promotion and protection of children's rights at the national level. It is the aim of this chapter to consider the emergence of such institutions around the world, considering their diverse form and approach set against the international standards. It seeks to explain the unique role played by national children's rights institutions, identifying the features that are instrumental for effective promotion and protection of children's rights at a national level.

The chapter has two principal parts. The first part considers the international standards, specifically the Paris Principles which are the standard bearer for NHRIs accredited via the Global Alliance for National Human Rights Institutions (GANHRI). It then moves onto consider the standards specific to national children's rights institutions under the CRC before analysing the emergence of national independent children's rights institutions around the world.

## 2.2 International Standards on National Human Rights Institutions

The Vienna Declaration and Programme of Action, adopted by the Second World Conference on Human Rights in 1993, restated the global community's commitment to human rights and called for universal ratification of all human rights treaties, as well as the strengthening of mechanisms and programmes designed to advance the enforcement, implementation and co-ordination of human rights protection at the international and national levels (UN, 1993). Although NHRIs had been established long before the Vienna Declaration, the Second World Conference is largely credited with their increase in number and strength and in various ways since that time—through General Assembly resolutions and treaty body recommendations—the UN has repeatedly reaffirmed support for NHRIs (Sidoti, 2011, pp. 93–94). In December 1993, the General Assembly adopted a set of principles relating to the status of national institutions for the promotion and protection of human rights (UN General Assembly, 1993). Known as the Paris Principles, these were agreed to be the standards that such institutions should meet. The Principles were drafted in a workshop convened by the UN Centre for Human Rights in 1991 and both their timing—they were agreed prior to the 'rush of interest' in such institutions—and origin—they were drafted by the institutions themselves—added to their credibility and importance (Sidoti, 2011, pp. 95–96). The Vienna Declaration expressly encouraged the 'establishment and strengthening of national institutions' having regard to the Paris Principles, and it reaffirmed their 'important and constructive role' in the promotion and protection of human rights, specifically, their advisory work, their role in remedying human rights violations, in the dissemination of human rights information, and in human rights education (UN, 1993, para. 36).

The Paris Principles (para. 3) highlight that NHRIs should be directed at both the protection of human rights, including receiving, investigating and resolving complaints, mediating conflicts and monitoring activities, and the promotion of human rights, through education, outreach, engaging with the media, training and capacity building, as well as advising and assisting Government. They set minimum criteria that must be met for NHRIs to reach the international standard. First, they include requirements regarding the mandate and competence of such institutions which must be based on universal human rights norms and standards and be as broad as possible. Second, they require NHRIs to have a level of autonomy from Government, including in relation to financial control and third, their independence must be guaranteed by statute or in the Constitution. Fourth, NHRIs must have adequate resources and infrastructure to fulfil their mandate, including adequate funding and fifth, they must have sufficient powers to ensure the fulfilment of their functions, including powers of investigation. Finally, their composition and appointment must be such as to ensure pluralistic representation of those involved in the promotion and protection of human rights.

Goodman and Pegram (2011, p. 1) noted that the previous two decades had witnessed a proliferation of national human rights commissions and human rights ombudsmen across ‘every continent and subregion of the world’. This development has been supported at international level by the Global Alliance of National Human Rights Institutions (GANHRI, https://ganhri.org/), established in 1993 to promote and strengthen NHRIs in line with the Paris Principles. Accreditation provides a system of international recognition for NHRIs that supports validated compliance with the Paris Principles, and by January 2021, 127 NHRIs had been accredited by GANHRI. Under its General Observations, the Alliance offers guidance on the interpretation and application of the Paris Principles, designed to achieve and promote greater compliance among NHRIs with these international standards.

## 2.3 CRC Standards on Independent Human Rights Institutions for Children

In parallel with these developments, the adoption of the UN Convention on the Rights of the Child (CRC) and the establishment of the UN Committee on the Rights of the Child (the CRC Committee) placed children’s rights firmly on the international stage. Building on the emphasis in the 1993 World Conference on both children’s rights (UN, 1993, paras. 45–53) and on national human rights institutions (UN, 1993, para. 36), the Committee adopted standards on independent human rights institutions for children in 2002. In its second General Comment, the Committee advised that ‘every state needs an independent human rights institution with responsibility for promoting and protecting children’s rights’ (CRC Committee, 2002, para. 7) and it framed its General Comment as a way to encourage the establishment of such institutions in line with the Paris Principles and the Convention on the Rights of the Child. In line with the Paris Principles, the Committee stated that NHRIs should if possible be ‘constitutionally entrenched’, and at the very least ‘legislatively mandated’ (2002, para. 8). Their mandate should include ‘as broad a scope as possible for promoting and protecting human rights’, incorporating the CRC and its Optional Protocols so that children’s human rights are effectively covered (CRC Committee, 2002, para. 8). In line with the Paris Principles' requirements of independence, autonomy, adequate resourcing and pluralistic representation, the General Comment highlights the particular elements of NHRIs that address their accessibility and relevance to children. In particular, the Committee recommends that such institutions 'reach out to all groups of children' particularly the most disadvantaged and the vulnerable, in line with Article 2 of the CRC (non-discrimination) (2002, para. 15) and recommend that they should have a key role to play in promoting respect for the views of all children in matters that affect them, consistent with Article 12. Specifically, the Committee (2002, para. 16) notes,

> Institutions must ensure that they have direct contact with children and that children are appropriately involved and consulted. Children's councils, for example, could be created as advisory bodies for NHRIs to facilitate the participation of children in matters of concern to them.

They should have 'specially tailored consultation programmes and imaginative communication strategies' in order to ensure full compliance with Article 12 (CRC Committee, 2002, para. 17).

The General Comment provides that NHRIs must have the power to 'consider individual complaints and petitions and carry out investigations, including those submitted on behalf of or directly by children', and have the necessary powers to do so effectively (2002, para. 13). They should also have the power to 'support children taking cases to court', both initiating litigation on behalf of children and intervening as a third party where necessary to advise the court about the human rights issues in the case (CRC Committee, 2002, para. 14). The General Comment also details the type of activities that NHRIs should undertake in the promotion and protection of children's rights. This inexhaustive list includes undertaking investigations and conducting inquiries into children's rights, preparing opinions and recommendations at the request of authorities and on their own volition, keeping law and policy under review from a children's rights perspective and promoting the harmonisation with the Convention of law, regulation and practice. The Committee also highlights the important role NHRIs play in monitoring Government implementation of the Convention and recommends that they ensure the impact of law and policy on children is carefully considered 'from development to implementation and beyond' (2002, para. 19). Specific activities relating to Articles 3 and 12 of the Convention are set out, along with recommendations in line with Article 42 of the Convention that the mandate of NHRIs should include activities to promote and advance awareness of children's rights, both among children themselves, professionals working with and for children and the public at large (2002, para. 19). Importantly, the Committee makes a distinction between the role played by NHRIs and that of Government and civil society organisations and while it encourages close collaboration with the latter, with respect to Government it cautions that institutions must remain 'entirely free to set their own agenda and determine their own activities' (2002, para. 25). International and regional consultation and co-operation is encouraged as such opportunities help NHRIs to 'learn from each other's experience, collectively strengthen each other's positions and contribute to resolving human rights problems affecting both countries and regions' (2002, para. 29).

It is apparent from General Comment No. 2 that there is a strong coherence between the requirements set down in the Paris Principles with respect to NHRIs and those articulated by the CRC Committee in respect of independent human rights institutions for children. The model set out by the Committee is an adapted form of NHRI (it uses this nomenclature throughout) in line with the specific circumstances of children and children's rights in the CRC (Lansdown, 2020, p. 499). Although the Committee notes that '[s]pecialist independent human rights institutions for children, ombudspersons or commissioners for children's rights have been established in a growing number of States parties', it makes the pragmatic observation that, 'where resources are limited ... development of a broad-based NHRI that includes a specific focus on children is likely to constitute the best approach' (2020, para. 6). Whatever its form, according to the Committee, the institution should be able, independently and effectively, to monitor, promote and protect children's rights'; the mainstreaming of the promotion and protection of children's rights should be essential; and all human rights institutions should work closely together to this end (2002, para. 7).

## 2.4 Strengths and Weaknesses of NHRIs for Children

The first national independent human rights institution for children—established in Norway in 1981—substantially pre-dated both the Paris Principles and the Committee's General Comment (Seneviratne, 2001,

p. 219). The duty of the 'Barneombud' was to promote children's interests in relation to public and private authorities, to conduct investigations on their own initiative or at the request of others and to ensure that legislation protecting children's interests was observed. An early evaluation of the office—in 1993—found that the existence of the Ombudsman had helped to 'put children on the political agenda', had been instrumental in developing an acceptance that 'children are entitled to be heard and that they have their own rights' (Seneviratne, 2001, p. 219).

Whether framed as a commissioner or an ombudsman for children, the model has since diffused across European and international boundaries—adapting to the legal, social, and economic landscape of countries ranging from Austria, Sweden and Ireland, to Spain, the United Kingdom and New Zealand (Seneviratne, 2001, pp. 219–221; Thomas et al., 2011, pp. 436–437). As offices have 'mushroom[ed]' (Thomas, 2011, p. 279) across Europe, they have been modified to fit national frameworks (Seneviratne, 2001, p. 222). This has translated into variations in the shape, power, and role of the institutions (Thomas, 2011; Thomas et al., 2011, p. 431). For instance, depending on the breadth of the mandate, some institutions adopt a proactive and reactive role—pursuing strategic objectives *and* responding to individual complaints (Rees, 2010, p. 434; Thomas, 2011). Some are shaped as separate entities, others are entwined within or integrated into existing NHRI structures (Seneviratne, 2001, pp. 222–223). The Council of Europe (2019) has acknowledged the 'diversity of Ombudsman institutions', while emphasising that their adoption and implementation must be underpinned by, and align with, certain core principles. Their role is wide-ranging and varied and in line with the vision set out by the CRC Committee in 2002, includes (among others): influencing law and policy; facilitating the voice of the child; monitoring activities and ensuring effective use of resources; advocacy; co-ordinating relevant services; data collection and publication; and investigating individual complaints (CRC Committee, 2002; Miljeteig, 2005; Rees, 2010; Seneviratne, 2001). Progress has been uneven internationally, however, with limited evidence in the African region to date of dedicated institutions for children (Sloth-Nielsen, 2020).

NHRIs have been characterised as the 'bridge between the international and domestic systems of human rights protection', instrumental to the implementation of human rights obligations (Carver, 2010, p. 1). Since its adoption, the CRC has proven to be at the fulcrum of NHRIs for children, expressly enshrined in the underpinning legislation in some countries (Thomas et al., 2011, p. 429). A fundamental aspect of the role of NHRIs for children in practice is their work to ensure compliance with the obligations of the CRC—promoting the harmonisation of national legislation with the Convention and embracing the implementation of its provisions (CRC Committee, 2002, para. 19; Doek, 2008, p. 6). They have a key role in strengthening the necessary infrastructure for the implementation of the CRC, including raising public awareness and ensuring the necessary resources are in place (Doek, 2008, p. 14). Lansdown's analysis of existing institutions highlights weaknesses in the mandates of many offices, including gaps or limitations in their establishing legislation which many were keen to address (Lansdown, 2020, p. 499). However, she notes that a survey by ENOC, the European Network of Ombudspersons for Children, of its 37 members found that all but one confirmed that they were able to act and speak out on any matter concerning children's rights, while noting also that independence is often more effectively determined by the level of financial autonomy that the institution enjoys both with regard to the sufficiency of resources and its control over how the budget is spent (Lansdown, 2020, pp. 500–501). A UNICEF survey of NHRIs, which identified a trend towards the integration of different human rights institutions in the interests of cost-saving or sectoral consolidation, noted that in most cases strong advocacy by children's rights advocates has meant that such challenges have been withstood (Sedletzki, 2012).

Many NHRIs for children combine a proactive with a reactive role, targeting the long-term enhancement of children's rights (pursuing strategic objectives) and responding to individual cases simultaneously (Thomas, 2011, p. 283). The role of each national institution is shaped by the legislative landscape—hinging on the scope of the afforded powers (Rees, 2010). This is effectively illustrated by the inconsistency surrounding the potential for NHRIs to receive and investigate individual complaints (Rees, 2010). Their mandate varies across boundaries, for example, the investigation of individual cases is a defining role of NHRIs in certain countries (such as New Zealand; and the majority of countries in Europe, including Ireland's Ombudsman for Children), with the position starkly different in others (such as the Children's Commissioner in England and in Scotland) where such institutions are not permitted to consider individual complaints or to respond to specific breaches of children's rights (Rees, 2010; Thomas, 2011, pp. 281–282). The Paris Principles do not explicitly oblige NHRIs to adopt a reactive approach and investigate individual cases (Rees, 2010, p. 419). In fact, arguments against their investigative role have centred around costly resources associated with this model and the potential 'detrimental' (Rees, 2010, p. 420) impact on the strategic working of the institution, given the risk that it may become 'engulfed' (Innocenti Centre, 1997, p. 7) by casework (Rees, 2010). However, the CRC Committee is firm in the view that NHRIs should be empowered to receive and respond to individual complaints—equipped with the power to question witnesses and compel and examine evidence (2002, para. 13) and in this respect, the General Comment went further than the Paris Principles by arguing that individual complaints mechanisms should be 'embedded in the mandates of all such institutions' (Lansdown, 2020, p. 502). At the same time, criticism has been made of the fact that in many cases, the complaint mechanisms of NHRIs for children are 'largely quasi-judicial' (Sedletzki, 2012, p. 25), meaning that although institutions can make recommendations on foot of a complaint or investigation, they do not have powers of enforcement comparable with courts. Chirwa (2015) found this to be a particular problem in African models. Lansdown makes the important observation that in this context, much will depend on 'the quality of their research, their perceived independence, and the reputation of the institution' (2020, p. 503). Similarly, as Sloth Nielsen notes, these recommendations get enforced through 'political pressure, political agents such as a minister, president or parliament, or action to enforce its decision through ordinary courts' (Sloth Nielsen, 2019, p. 61). The Committee's failure to recommend that NHRIs should be able to make binding decisions is thus a limitation insofar as institutions without this power have restricted capacity to respond to individual cases. In this respect, Rees considers that the 'power envisaged by the UN Committee does fall short of the expectations of the Paris Principles for NHRIs with a quasi-judicial competence' (2010, p. 420).

Rees (2010) has emphasised the centrality of NHRIs for children in dealing with individual cases, supporting the Committee in its recognition of this role as an essential function of such institutions (CRC Committee, 2005a, para. 7; 2005b, para. 10). While Lansdown shares the view that 'effective remedies for rights violations is fundamental to the realisation of human rights', she notes that the majority but not all NHRIs for children have powers to investigate (2020, p. 502). Rees (2010) argues that responding to individual complaints (whether through advocacy or via an investigative role) is vital in tackling violations of children's rights and potentially invoking systemic reform. Broader change may stem from this responsive (and individualised) approach, with Rees (2010, p. 434) arguing that it is 'possible for proactive and reactive functions to work in tandem'. Responding to individual complaints enables institutions to directly target (and react to) infringements of children's rights while adopting a proactive approach in preventing repeat violations in the future (Rees, 2010, p. 434). Thus, even without powers of enforcement, individual complaints can play an important role in highlighting patterns of systemic rights violations and in connecting with advocacy work, they can serve to support the institution's broader mandate (Lansdown, 2020, p. 503), ultimately facilitating the implementation of the CRC (Rees, 2010, p. 434). Rees (2010, p. 434) also reflects on the applicability of this entwined function of dealing with individual complaints irrespective of contextual (social, political, economic) factors. He points to the relevancy of this in countries with either a robust or weak children's rights framework where it can provide an effective mechanism for responding to violations of children's rights (where an alternative is lacking) and ensure the compliance of Government and public bodies with their relevant obligations (Rees, 2010, p. 434). In sum, it is recommended that NHRIs for children are established (or extended) to make provision for the entwined power to respond to individual cases (Rees, 2010, p. 434). Affording such institutions with some element of quasi-judicial competence would strengthen these institutions as mechanisms promoting and protecting children's rights (Rees, 2010, p. 433).

In reality, of those institutions able to receive complaints, the 2012 UNICEF survey found that their specific mandates vary significantly with some limitations on who could complain and on what subject (Sedletzki, 2012). Moreover, Lansdown (2020) notes little evidence of systematic evaluation of the effectiveness of complaints procedures by NHRIs for children, either with regard to the accessibility of the procedure or the outcomes. She also highlights the concern that the vast majority of complaints are made by parents rather than children, a pattern that she notes is 'widely replicated' across institutions (Lansdown, 2020, p. 503), in a failure to make complaints mechanisms genuinely accessible to children. Institutions themselves struggle to reach out to children, and children themselves face multiple barriers, including a lack of awareness about available remedies, lack of knowledge as to how to access these remedies, and a lack of trust or confidence that they will be taken seriously if they do complain (Kilkelly, forthcoming). The power of NHRIs for children to initiate or intervene in legal action on behalf of children is a largely unexplored but important issue in this context (Sloth Nielsen, 2019).

Although the fundamental role of NHRIs for children lies at the national level, the impact of these institutions also extends to the international context (Carver, 2010; Doek, 2008). The CRC Committee has highlighted the importance of engagement with treaty monitoring, recommending that NHRIs for children should contribute independently to this process, monitoring the integrity of government reporting (2002, para. 20). The Committee has also recommended that NHRIs for children bring to this process information on their legislative basis and activity so that the compliance of the institution can be considered by the Committee in its assessment of state party implementation (2002, para. 21). NHRIs for children can also assist the Committee in monitoring the implementation of the CRC in their respective countries by submitting periodic reports and enhancing co-operation through robust regional networks (Doek, 2008, para. 3.3.3). Assessing the impact of NHRIs for children is important, accounting for both their proactive and reactive elements (Thomas, 2011, p. 283). Thomas (2011) has illustrated the challenges associated with this impact assessment, including confirming the specific objectives which vary depending on the power and function envisaged and afforded by the country's adaption of the model. Further challenges lie in identifying suitable indicators, data collection (barriers relating to the availability of/access to data), and attributing cause and effect (Thomas, 2011, p. 284). Although evaluation is vitally important, Doek (2008, pp. 13–14) points to the challenges of measuring the impact of certain key activities, such as awareness raising and advocacy. The establishment of an NHRI for children indicates that existing structures are inadequate in promoting and protecting children's rights (Seneviratne, 2001, p. 222). A key component of the Paris Principles is the functional independence of such institutions from government, an approach adopted across Europe, with few exceptions (Thomas, 2011, p. 281). Independence is an essential characteristic and key objective of NHRIs (Miljeteig, 2005; Smith, 2006). While the 'unique position' of NHRIs within the conceptual space between government and civil society is advantageous in the promotion and protection of children's rights (for instance, in influencing policy and engaging with NGOs), building relationships with these bodies while maintaining independence can pose a challenge (Smith, 2006).

There has been much inconsistency surrounding the position of institutions as separate specialised bodies *or* integrated within existing broader institutions (Doek, 2008; Seneviratne, 2001, pp. 222–223; Thomas, 2011, p. 282). Some countries (including Iceland, Norway and Sweden) have adopted independent models, others (such as Spain and Portugal) have enshrined specialist units within general human rights or ombudsman offices (Seneviratne, 2001, p. 223). The CRC Committee has supported the development of separate independent monitoring bodies, such as Children's Ombudspersons or Commissioners (CRC Committee, 2002) and although both the Committee and the Paris Principles recognise the centrality of independence, neither has offered guidance on the specific shape of such independence (Doek, 2008, p. 9). NHRIs for children require a robust legal basis, with its mandate and powers having the scope to enable its independence (CRC Committee, 2002, paras. 8–9; Doek, 2008, p. 9). This independence hinges upon adequate infrastructure and sufficient resources (CRC Committee, 2002, para. 6). On a practical level, limited resources may pose barriers to the formation of such freestanding institutions (CRC Committee, 2002, para. 6). The Committee recognises the subsequent need for a 'broad-based' NHRI with a specific division or commissioner targeting children's rights (2002, para. 6). Seneviratne (2001) has argued that there is potential for NHRIs for children to meet their objectives while interwoven within existing structures.

There are advantages and disadvantages to both positions (Seneviratne, 2001). The institution as a separate entity can ensure that children's rights are consistently prioritised, with the child perspective at the fulcrum of all its activities (Seneviratne, 2001). They provide separate resources for children's needs, while also providing a distinct channel to support the voice of young people (Seneviratne, 2001). On the other hand, dedicated offices bring visibility and an accessibility to children themselves, which is particularly important given the traditional failure to recognise children as subjects of human rights (Lansdown, 2020). Children may face barriers accessing mainstream institutions, and their voice and needs may become lost within broader human rights issues (Lansdown, 2020; Seneviratne, 2001).

On the other hand, integrated institutions can allow for 'greater cross-sectoral advocacy and monitoring' (Lansdown, 2020, p. 502) and serve to reinforce that children, like adults, are rights holders entitled to claim their rights against the state. This is especially true where human rights institutions have constitutional standing, that a dedicated children's institution may not enjoy. Whereas dedicated offices can risk marginalising children's rights issues, integrated children's rights institutions may prevent this (Seneviratne, 2001). Thomas et al. (2011) conducted interviews with members of ENOC, finding that the majority (14 out of the 23 interviewed) favoured a freestanding children's rights institution, primarily due to the risk of children's rights issues becoming lost within the mainstream institutions. The benefit of integrated institutions in facilitating the exchange of information, strategies and perspectives, was notably recognised (Thomas et al., 2011).

UNICEF published a global study on independent human rights institutions for children in 2012, identifying elements which underpin their effectiveness in the realisation of children's rights (Sedletzki, 2012). Independence was identified as an important feature, potentially impacting the scope for direct engagement with children, and the willingness of individuals to file complaints (Sedletzki, 2012). The legal recognition of NHRIs for children strengthens their status and legitimacy, whereas financial dependence may be necessary where there are limited resources (Sedletzki, 2012). The second element recognised was child participation, requiring measures to facilitate proactive engagement with children and accessible channels through which children can file complaints and raise concerns (Sedletzki, 2012). The active participation of children in the activities of these institutions was promoted, while measures are also needed to raise awareness and enhance accessibility (Sedletzki, 2012). The third identified element was the ability of the institution to receive complaints on children's rights issues, the potential for which is dependent upon the scope of the legislative mandate and afforded powers (Sedletzki, 2012). Finally, the study emphasised the importance of international engagement, which is an important source of support for institutions which may be somewhat isolated on a national level (Sedletzki, 2012). Structures facilitating international engagement (such as ENOC) enable concerns to be addressed and ideas and perspectives to be shared (Sedletzki, 2012).

The case for a dedicated human rights institution for children has been well articulated (CRC Committee, 2002; Lansdown, 2020; Sloth Nielsen, 2019). Apart from the important role that NHRIs play in the promotion and protection of children's rights, the marginalisation and vulnerability of children means that they can be powerless, invisible and voiceless in the face of adversity, when they are denied their rights, and in the political process, where key decisions as to law, policy and budgets are made (Seneviratne, 2001, pp. 221–222). Accessibility of an NHRI to children is key to its effectiveness as well as to its compliance with the CRC, and in this regard an NHRI's commitment to child participation needs to apply 'both to the ways in which they conduct their activities and to the nature of the work they undertake' (Lansdown, 2020, p. 504). As a measure of its importance, institutions have requirements around child participation written into their mandate in different ways. In practice, two approaches are evident—some offices have permanent advisory groups to inform the priorities of the office and to ensure their work is connected to children's lived experiences of their rights. Others undertake ad hoc consultations with children, to ensure that specific programmes or pieces of advocacy are informed by the views and perspectives of the children affected. Many NHRIs for children engage creatively and systematically with children in this regard, ensuring that the diversity and heterogeneity of children's experiences are represented by including children of different ages, backgrounds and circumstances in their work. As Lansdown (2020, p. 506) notes, this work has 'intrinsic value' in ensuring that children's voices are heard and taken into account while it also provides leadership to Government and other organisations, helping to demonstrate that children's participation can be mainstreamed in decision-making. Despite significant progress and good practice examples, however, there is potential for most NHRIs for children to explore 'far more radical engagement of children', including their integration into management decision-making and setting of strategic priorities (Lansdown, 2020, pp. 508–509).

## 2.5 Conclusion

The international standards—both the Paris Principles and the CRC General Comment—set clear expectations regarding the standing, resourcing and functioning of NHRIs for children. Although these are inconsistent or insufficiently robust in some respects—for example, with regard to requiring a dedicated office for children's rights and making recommendations arising out of investigations or complaints legally binding—the standards are clear with regard to key elements of independence and autonomy, resourcing and mandate. They are equally clear on elements of accessibility to children and the importance of ensuring children's voices are integrated into activities and priorities. While the proliferation of NHRIs for children is to be welcomed, it is important to ensure that focus is maintained equally on the imperatives to protect—through the handling of complaints and accessing legal remedies—as well as to promote children's rights through the softer approaches of education and public awareness. Further work is required to ensure that the standards keep pace with the development and experience of children's rights institutions and evaluations of their effectiveness.

Having set out the international standards to be met by NHRIs for children, the next chapter will introduce the Irish Ombudsman for Children. The chapters that follow will then illustrate, with regard to the activities and achievements of the approach taken primarily during the first decade of the institution, the extent to which the strengths and weaknesses identified here are evident from the Irish experience.

## References


Carver, R. (2010). A new answer to an old question: National human rights institutions and the domestication of international law. *Human Rights Law Review, 10*(1), 1–32.

Chirwa, D. (2015). *Monitoring and accountability mechanisms for the implementation of children's rights in Africa* (Working paper commissioned by the African Child Policy Forum).

Council of Europe. (2019). *Protection, promotion and development of the Ombudsman institution*. Council of Europe. Available at: https://rm.coe.int/ombudsman-institution-en-web/16809f667f. Accessed 15 Apr 2021.

Doek, J. E. (2008). *Independent human rights institutions for children* (Innocenti Working Paper No. 2008-06). UNICEF Innocenti Research Centre.

Global Alliance of National Human Rights Institutions (GANHRI). https://ganhri.org/. Accessed 8 Apr 2021.

Goodman, R., & Pegram, T. (Eds.). (2011). *Human rights, state compliance, and social change: Assessing national human rights institutions*. Cambridge University Press.

Innocenti Centre. (1997). *Ombudswork for children*. UNICEF, Innocenti Digest.

Kilkelly, U. (forthcoming). Children's rights to access justice at international level: Challenge and opportunity. In M. Paré, M. Bruning, C. Siffrein-Blanc, & M. Moreau, M. (Eds.), *Children's Access to Justice: A Critical Assessment*. Intersentia.

Lansdown, G. (2020). National human rights institutions for children. In J. Todres & S. King (Eds.), *The Oxford handbook of children's rights law* (pp. 495–512). Oxford University Press.

Miljeteig, P. (2005). *Children's Ombudsman: Save the Children Norway's experiences with supporting and cooperating with independent institutions protecting children's rights, vol 1.* Save the Children Norway.

Rees, O. (2010). Dealing with individual cases: An essential role for national human rights institutions for children? *The International Journal of Children's Rights, 18*(3), 417–436.

Sedletzki, V. (2012). *Championing children's rights: A global study of independent human rights institutions for children—Summary report.* Innocenti Publications.

Seneviratne, M. (2001). Ombudsman's section. *The Journal of Social Welfare & Family Law, 23*(2), 217–225.

Sidoti, C. (2011). National human rights institutions and the international human rights system. In R. Goodman & T. Pegram (Eds.), *Human rights, state compliance, and social change: Assessing national human rights institutions* (pp. 93–123). Cambridge University Press.

Sloth Nielsen, J. (2019). Monitoring and implementation of children's rights. In U. Kilkelly & T. Liefaard (Eds.), *International human rights of children* (pp. 31–64). Springer Nature.

Sloth-Nielsen, J. (2020). The role of national human rights institutions in enhancing the impact of children's rights reporting in Africa. In R. Miamingi (Ed.), *State party reporting and the realisation of children's rights in Africa* (pp. 283–306). Pretoria University Law Press.

Smith, A. (2006). The unique position of national human rights institutions: A mixed blessing. *Human Rights Quarterly, 28*, 904–946.

Thomas, N. (2011). The role and impact of independent children's rights institutions in the UK and Europe. *Journal of Social Welfare and Family Law, 33*(3), 279–288.

Thomas, N., Hanson, K., & Gran, B. (2011). An independent voice for children's rights in Europe? The role of independent children's rights institutions in the EU. *The International Journal of Children's Rights, 19*(3), 429–449.

UN. (1993). Vienna Declaration and Programme of Action, adopted by the World Conference on Human Rights in Vienna on 25 June 1993.

UN Committee on the Rights of the Child. (2002). *General Comment No. 2 (2002): The Role of Independent National Human Rights Institutions in the Promotion and Protection of the Rights of the Child*, 15 November 2002, CRC/GC/2002/2.

UN Convention on the Rights of the Child (CRC). (1989).

UN Committee on the Rights of the Child. (2005a). *Concluding observations: Sweden*, 30 March 2005, CRC/C/15/Add.248.

UN Committee on the Rights of the Child. (2005b). *Concluding observations: Finland*, 20 October 2005, CRC/C/15/Add.272.

UN General Assembly. (1993). Principles relating to the status of national institutions (Paris Principles). UN Doc. A/RES/48/134.

CHAPTER 3

# The Irish Model—The Ombudsman for Children

**Abstract** Ireland introduced its national human rights institution for children with the enactment in 2004 of the Ombudsman for Children Act 2002. The development was a clear political response to a series of child abuse scandals at the national level and Ireland's ratification of the United Nations Convention on the Rights of the Child in 1992 and its first appearance before the Committee on the Rights of the Child in 1998. These events highlighted the need for an independent national body established through the enactment of legislation, with the power and authority to protect and promote children's rights. Under the 2002 Act, the Ombudsman for Children is created as an independent office, accountable to parliament, resourced and empowered in line with the expectations of the Paris Principles and General Comment No. 2 of the United Nations Committee on the Rights of the Child. This chapter presents the legislative basis of the Ombudsman for Children, traces its origins and background, and then considers the extent to which it meets the international standards for NHRIs for children.

**Keywords** Ombudsman for children · Advocacy · Legislation · International standards · Children's rights promotion and protection · Investigation



U. Kilkelly and E. Logan, *National Independent Human Rights Institutions for Children*,
https://doi.org/10.1007/978-3-030-80275-2_3

## 3.1 Introduction

In 1992, Ireland ratified the Convention on the Rights of the Child (CRC, 1989) providing impetus to renewed efforts, in law and policy, to improve the treatment of children in harmony with the Convention (Kilkelly, 2015). Following on from a series of national reports into child abuse and ill-treatment, including a scandal that had collapsed the Government, Ireland committed to the introduction of a national institution for children with a range of powers to protect and promote children's rights. Although the result of intense lobbying by Ireland's civil society groups, notably the newly formed Children's Rights Alliance, the Ombudsman for Children Act 2002 was also influenced by Ireland's appearance before the Committee on the Rights of the Child (the CRC Committee) in 1998. The Act that came into force in 2004 established an independent institution for children, with an investigation power at its cornerstone, combined with a range of proactive duties to promote children's rights through research, awareness raising, education and advocacy, all from a children's rights perspective. In 2004, Emily Logan, Ireland's first Ombudsman for Children, was appointed to the role for the first of her two terms of office. The second office holder, Dr. Niall Muldoon was appointed in 2015.

The Ombudsman for Children is established under the legislation as an independent office, resourced and empowered in line with the expectations of the Paris Principles (UN General Assembly, 1993) and General Comment No. 2 of the United Nations Committee on the Rights of the Child (CRC Committee, 2002). The aim of this chapter is to introduce the Irish model, tracing its origins and background, while analysing the extent to which it meets the international standards set out in Chapter 2.

## 3.2 Background to the Establishment of the Ombudsman for Children

### 3.2.1 *Ireland's History of Child Abuse*

By the time Ireland had ratified the United Nations Convention on the Rights of the Child (1989) in 1992, a growing number of high-profile child abuse scandals had started to make clear that there was a very significant gap between the Convention's standards and many children's lived experiences of their rights in Ireland. Although Ireland's history of child abuse is now well documented (Kilkelly, 2012; O'Mahony & Kilkelly, 2014; Raftery, 1999), the apology of An Taoiseach Bertie Ahern in 1999 to the victims of childhood abuse (RTE, 1999), and the establishment of a large national inquiry into institutional abuse (Commission to Inquire into Child Abuse, 2009), laid bare the state's appalling failure to protect the rights of children (McGarry, 2019). It was thus against this backdrop that proposals began to be made to introduce a national human rights institution for children. Two specific events were particularly catalytic in this regard. The first was the publication of the Kilkenny Incest Investigation (McGuinness, 1993), which concerned the state's failure to protect a child from 15 years of physical and sexual abuse by her father and the second, of more political significance, involved the delay in the extradition of Father Brendan Smyth, subsequently convicted of multiple cases of child sexual abuse in Northern Ireland, which led to the collapse of the Irish Government in 1994 (*Irish Times*, 2015). These events attracted national and international media attention (Donnelly, 2016) and ignited public outrage (Clarity, 1993), which together presented a watershed moment in the national response to the protection of children.

The first record of parliamentary debate about the introduction of an Ombudsman for Children in Ireland was in 1995, when the Government was questioned about setting up an institution for children similar to that in Norway, Sweden and other countries (Dáil Éireann Debate, February 1995). In 1997, a statement was made by the then Minister that he was fully committed to the principle of establishing an ombudsman for children 'to ensure the responsiveness of services to the needs of children and to promote their rights' (Dáil Éireann Debate, March 1997). However, a change of Government led to reprioritisation in favour of setting up a Social Services Inspectorate (O'Morain, 1998) and although it was five more years before the legislation establishing the Ombudsman for Children was passed, the intervening period presented an important opportunity to build consensus on the form this institution would take.

### 3.2.2 *Advocacy, Research and the Role of Civil Society*

Following Ireland's ratification of the CRC, eleven non-governmental organisations came together in 1995 to form the Children's Rights Alliance (the Alliance) to collaborate on the promotion and implementation of the Convention in Ireland. At its inaugural annual general meeting, the Alliance agreed that one of its core aims should be the establishment of a new public office that could play a significant role in the implementation of the Convention and as a first step, the Alliance secured funding to undertake comparative research on the subject, bringing together governmental and non-governmental actors to form a steering group for the project (Cousins, 1996). The research included an exploration of the experience from countries with a broadly similar legal and socio-economic system to that of Ireland and it examined the national children's rights institutions in Norway, Sweden, Finland, British Columbia and New Zealand and the National Council on Children's Rights in Denmark (Cousins, 1996, p. 5). The report illustrates some of the tensions that existed at that time—it notes that the Government imperative was to respond to the public outrage about child abuse, while the NGO motivation, guided by the Convention, was focused on a more empowering approach to secure rights for *all* children. Ireland's general public services ombudsman institution, had been in place since 1984, and as a model with which Government was familiar, this was its preferred approach. A supportive visit to Ireland by the Ombudsman for Children from Norway, including a meeting with the Minister, resulted in a commitment to incorporate some of the features of the Norwegian institution into the Irish model (Coulter, 1999). As a result, it was agreed to combine the functions of children's rights promotion (including awareness raising, legislative advice and education) with that of protection (including the investigation of complaints) (Cousins, 1996, pp. 71–72). In line with international standards, the research recommended that the office be established on a statutory basis, independent of government departments and accountable to the Oireachtas (Parliament). It also recommended that it should set in place procedures to consult with children in relation to all aspects of its work and be empowered to take legal action before the Irish or European courts (Cousins, 1996, p. 71). Given the scale of concerns about the treatment of children at the time, the Alliance also recommended the need to develop a range of effective governmental structures, rather than assuming that the new body would be a panacea for existing problems (Cousins, 1996, p. 72). Interestingly, in light of the scale of this ambition, in her closing statement of the parliamentary debate on the legislation to enact the Ombudsman for Children, the relevant Minister cautioned that the Ombudsman will not solve every problem, they will.

not protect every child or family because he or she will not be able to visit every home or walk down every street (Seanad Éireann Debate, April 2002)

### 3.2.3 *The Role of the UN Committee on the Rights of the Child*

International influence on the national development to introduce Ireland's national human rights institution for children came during the consideration of Ireland's first state party report to the UN Committee on the Rights of the Child (CRC Committee, 1996). The report detailed the legislative and other measures being taken to harmonise national law and policy with the Convention and it sought to demonstrate Ireland's political commitment to children's rights by being the first country in Europe to appoint a minister with special responsibility for children (CRC Committee, 1996, para. 51). When the state party delegation appeared before the Committee in 1998, there was some unexpected challenge by the Committee about Ireland's patronising approach to children, with concern expressed that there was a lot of talk of protection and not enough of empowerment (Smyth, 1998). The decision to prioritise a Social Services Inspectorate ahead of the creation of an Ombudsman for Children was criticised for this reason (Smyth, 1998). In its Concluding Observations, the Committee outlined a number of concerns, including the state party's fragmented approach to children, its lack of comprehensive national policy and the lack of co-ordination across government bodies in promoting and protecting the rights of the child (CRC Committee, 1998, paras. 6–10). While it welcomed the decision to establish the Social Services Inspectorate, the Committee expressed concern about the lack of an independent monitoring mechanism such as an Ombudsperson or a Child Rights Commissioner who would be accessible to children and would deal with complaints of violations of their rights and provide remedies (CRC Committee, 1998, para. 9). In this respect, the Committee recommended that the State party reconsider the establishment of an independent monitoring body to address children's rights violations (1998, para. 29). There seems little doubt that the introduction of the Ombudsman for Children legislation at a more accelerated pace than originally intended was as a result of the scathing criticism of the Irish Government by the Committee (Martin, 2004, p. 59).

### 3.2.4 *Further Influences on the Ombudsman for Children*

The strength of public reaction to Ireland's multiple child abuse scandals and effective national and international advocacy thus combined to galvanise political will in support of the national human rights institution for children. While international influences played a role in both prompting state action and informing the model ultimately adopted (Martin, 2004), the Ombudsman for Children Bill, introduced in 2002, also relied heavily on the existing public services Ombudsman, with which the legislature was very familiar (Ombudsman Act, 1980). Research indicates that parliamentary draftspersons had substantial difficulties defining the scope of the proposed powers and functions (Martin, 2004, p. 59), with concerns that the constitutional position of the family would be impacted if the legislative boundaries of the Ombudsman for Children were to impinge on the family's private sphere (Martin, 2004, pp. 59–60). While ultimately this concern was overcome, as later chapters indicate, this was not the last time that the Constitution would impact on the role of the Ombudsman for Children.

## 3.3 Ombudsman for Children Act 2002

By 2000, Government had approved the drafting of a Bill and appointed the parliamentary counsel with a commitment to publish later that year (Dáil Éireann Debate, May 2000). The principal functions were outlined as: the promotion of the welfare and rights of children and to act as a catalyst for change; to respond to individual complaints in relation to public, private and voluntary bodies, and the establishment of mechanisms through which there would be regular consultation with children and an advisory role to Government (Dáil Éireann Debate, May 2000). By early 2002, the Ombudsman for Children Bill was making its way through the upper house of parliament (Seanad Éireann Debate, April 2002) and the Ombudsman for Children was established as primary law, the Ombudsman for Children Act 2002, later that year.

In terms of institutional competence and responsibilities, the Ombudsman for Children is mandated to promote the rights and welfare of children and according to the legislation, has a very broad mandate, with multiple provisions specifying its sphere of competence and authority (e.g., Ombudsman for Children Act 2002, ss. 7–10, 13–15, 18–19).

This includes: the promotion of children's rights, including the provisions of the Convention and how those rights can be enforced, advising Government on the development and co-ordination of policy relating to children, and advising Government on any matter, including the probable effect on children of the implementation of any proposals for legislation, relating to the rights of children. In addition, the Ombudsman for Children may undertake, promote or publish research into any matter relating to the rights of children and this includes placing a special report before the Oireachtas (Parliament) (Ombudsman for Children Act, 2002, s. 7). Significantly, as is evident, the legislation uses the language of children's rights and in particular, the Ombudsman for Children has a duty to promote the rights and welfare of children (s. 7), highlighting issues of concern relating to the rights and welfare of children that are of concern to children themselves. In the examination and investigation of complaints under the Act, the Ombudsman must 'have regard to the best interests of the child concerned and shall, in so far as practicable, give due consideration, having regard to the age and understanding of the child, to his or her wishes' (s. 6(2)).

Independence is the distinguishing hallmark of the institution and is crucial to its successful operation (Martin, 2004, p. 61). Indeed, the legislation contains an express statement of institutional independence (s. 6), while it also provides that the office holder—the Ombudsman for Children—shall be appointed by a resolution being passed by both Houses of the Oireachtas (Parliament) , before formally being appointed by the Head of State, the President of Ireland (s. 4). The term of office is six years, with reappointment possible once only (s. 4). The Act guarantees five specific ways in which the Ombudsman for Children may expect to interact with and account to the Oireachtas (Parliament), as part of the public accountability of the role and the performance of its functions:

- First, the Ombudsman for Children must submit an annual report on the performance of their functions to be laid before each House of the Oireachtas (Parliament) (s. 13(7)).
- Second, following an investigation, if it appears to the Ombudsman for Children that the measures taken or proposed in response to a recommendation are not satisfactory, they may issue a special report on the case (s. 13(5)).

- Third, from time to time the Ombudsman for Children may cause 'such other reports' with respect to those functions as they think fit (s. 13(7)).
- Fourth, the Ombudsman for Children is expected to not only monitor legislation concerning the rights and welfare of children, but to monitor and review the operation of the Ombudsman for Children Act 2002, making recommendations to Government and/or the Oireachtas (Parliament) on any amendments required (s. 7(1)(h)).
- Finally, while the Ombudsman for Children may be called before an Oireachtas (parliamentary) committee to account for any statutory functions, there are express limitations on what the Ombudsman, as an independent officer of the State, may be required to address (s. 19(2)). The Ombudsman is only accountable to the Oireachtas (Parliament) with respect to the economic and efficient use of resources (s. 18).

In line with the Paris Principles' (UN General Assembly, 1993) principle of 'quasi-judicial competence', the Ombudsman for Children has the power to investigate individual complaints made by children or on behalf of children arising in the course of the administration of public bodies (ss. 8–9), and the institution has discretion over whether to initiate, continue or discontinue an investigation (s. 10). While the power to investigate is generally in response to an individual complaint, the Ombudsman for Children can also investigate on the basis of their own initiative where it appears in all the circumstances that this is warranted (s. 10(1)(a)). As noted above, the Ombudsman for Children may make a special report to parliament if it appears that the measures taken or proposed in response to any recommendation are not satisfactory (s. 13(5)).

While the power to investigate cases was a welcome addition to the powers of the institution, concern was expressed, in particular by civil society organisations and academics, that this could create difficulties in terms of case management, with a possible overwhelming of the new office by individual casework to the detriment of its other functions, in particular its more proactive or strategic activities (Martin, 2004). As is discussed later below, the integrated approach whereby matters that arise through the adjudication of individual complaints are used for broader advocacy and awareness raising or for more strategic approaches, has been an important hallmark of the Ombudsman's work. This has helped to strengthen its interactions with public bodies, enhancing its reputation among the public and ensuring that the experiences of children are brought to bear for the purposes of systemic reform.

### *3.3.1 Compatibility with International Standards*

Viewed against the international standards in Chapter 2, notably the Paris Principles and General Comment No. 2 of the Committee on the Rights of the Child (CRC Committee, 2002), the legislation establishing the Ombudsman for Children has many strengths. In line with the Paris Principles, the Ombudsman has institutional competence and a broad mandate encompassing both the promotion and the protection of children's rights. Its institutional independence is protected in various ways in legislation, though not in the Constitution, and its autonomous position as an independent body has been gradually and carefully consolidated. Although its independence in budgetary terms has been a subject of concern—its budget is set by the relevant government department and not by the Oireachtas (Parliament)—in all other respects, the independence and autonomy of the office are protected. For example, when the Irish Human Rights Commission was merged with the Equality Authority to form the Irish Human Rights and Equality Commission, the temptation to merge the Ombudsman for Children, evident in other jurisdictions, was resisted (Lansdown, 2020). The inclusion of the complaints handling mandate means that the Ombudsman for Children goes further than many NHRIs for children in meeting the requirements of the Paris Principles and General Comment No. 2 of the CRC Committee. The institution also has wide-ranging powers to both promote and protect the rights of the child through awareness raising, advising Government on matters of law and policy, and conducting both research and investigations relating to children's rights. Specific reference in the Act to the duty of the Ombudsman for Children to promote the rights of the child (s. 7) makes the rights-basis of the office very clear, while the duty to have regard to the best interests of the child and the right of the child to be heard in the conduct of complaints and investigations (s. 6(2)) reinforces this point.

That is not to say that the Irish model is fully compliant with international standards or indeed that the legislation on which it is based is without weaknesses or gaps. Concerns regarding several limitations in the Act were raised by members of the Oireachtas in both the lower and upper houses of the Oireachtas (Parliament) during the passage of the Ombudsman for Children Bill (Ombudsman for Children [OCO], 2005, p. 22). One concern was raised for instance with regard to the provision in the Act that provides for the exercise of a ministerial veto on investigations (OCO, 2005, p. 22). This was one of the provisions of the Ombudsman Act 1980, which allows for ministerial intervention and request to the Ombudsman to stop an investigation, which was replicated in the Ombudsman for Children's legislation. As Martin (2004) notes, one of the unsatisfactory aspects of the Ombudsman for Children Act had been its replication of this and other provisions relating to the carrying out of examinations and investigations. While it is worth noting that the provision has not been used since the inception of the public service Ombudsman's office in 1984, nonetheless, its repetition in the 2002 legislation was considered to be contrary to the spirit of independence set out in the Paris Principles (OCO, 2005, p. 27).

However, the most contested theme during the legislative process was the inclusion in the Act precluding the Ombudsman for Children from investigating an action 'taken in the administration of the prisons or other places for the custody or detention of children' (s. 11(1)(e)(iii)). With regard to children in prison, the Government explained that existing oversight mechanisms in the form of an Inspector of Prisons and the Council of Europe Committee on the Prevention of Torture would suffice to protect the rights of children in such situations (OCO, 2005, p. 24). Fortunately, this was overcome following advocacy by the Ombudsman for Children that brought about, through Ministerial Order, an amendment to allow children in prisons to access the complaint function of the office. Separately, the implementation of Government policy ending the detention of children in prison, as explained in Chapter 7 below, addressed the substantive concern.

In addition to concern about prisons, a high-profile case of a 14-year-old boy found in a coma in a police station, brought into sharp focus the vulnerability of children in other places of detention, especially police stations (Boucher Hayes, 2008). An Garda Síochána (the Irish police) play a key role in protecting the rights of children in conflict with the law, operating the national police diversion programme and with powers to arrest, detain and question children (Kilkelly, 2011). They also have powers in the context of child protection including emergency powers to remove children from parental custody under the Child Care Act 1991.

Early on, the Ombudsman for Children raised concern about the exclusion of children in these situations from the complaint function of the Ombudsman for Children (OCO, 2005, p. 25). Government explained that the reason for this exclusion was that children would have access to the new independent garda complaints mechanism (OCO, 2005, p. 25) and thus access to the Ombudsman was unnecessary. While the Garda Síochána Ombudsman Commission (GSOC) is now well established, questions remain about its accessibility to children. Nor is it apparent how it applies to the very sensitive area of child protection (Kilkelly & Forde, 2021).

The 2002 Act also precludes the Ombudsman for Children from investigating an action 'taken in the administration of the law relating to asylum, immigration, naturalisation or citizenship' (s. 11(1)(e)(i)). In the course of political debate, it was stated by the relevant Minister that 'children seeking refugee status or asylum can go to the Ombudsman for Children in relation to that process. It is only the decisions that are excluded' (Seanad Éireann Debate, February 2002). The Minister stated that the intention of this provision was to prevent any duplication of the refugee appeals process (OCO, 2005, p. 26). However, the interpretation of this provision has long been contested by the Ombudsman for Children (OCO, 2013, 2014). Following an attempted judicial review of the Direct Provision system and criticism by the judge of a lack of an independent complaints mechanism for children in such situations, the Government conceded and children can now submit complaints to the Ombudsman for Children (*C.A and T.A. v The Minister for Justice and others*).

The final investigatory exclusion is that the Ombudsman for Children cannot investigate any action undertaken by the Defence Forces. The legislation (s. 11(1)(b)) states that the Ombudsman for Children will not investigate an action which affects 'national security or military activity' (OCO, 2005, p. 26). In Ireland, children aged 17 can be and are recruited to the Irish Army. At the time the legislation was being drafted, the Government explained that the newly established Ombudsman for the Defence Forces could accept complaints from all recruits (OCO, 2005).

At the time of writing, therefore, all four exclusions of the investigatory remit are now either resolved through legislation, agreement on interpretation of the legislation, or through the development of other and new complaints handling mechanisms. While this is welcome, it is important that the legislation be kept under regular review so that its powers remain up to date to take account of contemporary challenges facing children's rights. In this regard, it is important that the Ombudsman for Children submitted to the Oireachtas (Parliament), after eight years of the institution, a report on the operation of the founding legislation (OCO, 2012), which found that in general the legislation was robust and functioned in a manner that had been critical to the establishment and development of a strong and credible institution (OCO, 2012, p. 4). At the same time, the report made several recommendations for reform, including an extension of the remit to include additional public bodies with functions relating primarily or exclusively to children which was done by virtue of the Ombudsman (Amendment) Act 2012 (OCO, 2013, p. 45). It also recommended expanding and clarifying the advisory functions, placing a new duty on public bodies to provide appropriate assistance and guidance to complainants, enhancing the powers of the Ombudsman for Children to ensure that public bodies comply with requests for information, documents or other records in the course of investigations and clarifying that the *in camera rule* should not operate in such a way as to frustrate statutory investigations under the Ombudsman for Children Act 2002 (OCO, 2012). To these recommendations could be added the addition of the remit to cover private institutions whose actions impact on children's rights, the inclusion of the power to submit amicus briefs in litigation concerning children's rights, and the introduction of a duty to have regard to the Ombudsman's recommendations during the enactment of legislation concerning children.

## 3.4 Conclusion

The Ombudsman for Children was introduced against the backdrop of child abuse inquiries and both public concern and political commitment to better ensure the protection of children. The role played by civil society—notably the Children's Rights Alliance—and a key intervention by the CRC Committee ensured that the body that was ultimately introduced was a robust, independent children's rights institution with a wide-ranging mandate and both proactive and reactive powers to protect and promote children's rights. This chapter has highlighted the extent to which the institution meets the international standards set out in Chapter 2, while identifying the importance of ensuring that the legislation is kept under review. In this regard, while certain loopholes in the legislation have now been closed, consideration should be given to extending the remit of the Ombudsman to cover private institutions which impact directly on children's lives and to strengthen its ability to contribute to litigation in cases that concern children's rights.

## References


Boucher Hayes, P. (2008, April 24). Death of Brian Rossiter in a Garda cell. *Magill Magazine*. Available at: https://magill.ie/archive/death-brian-rossiter-garda-cell. Accessed 31 Mar 2021.

*C.A and T.A. v The Minister for Justice and others* [2014] IEHC 532.

Child Care Act 1991.

Clarity, J. F. (1993, March 4). Rape-incest case in Ireland provokes furor. *New York Times*. Available at: https://www.nytimes.com/1993/03/04/world/rape-incest-case-in-ireland-provokes-furor.html. Accessed 31 Mar 2021.

Commission to Inquire into Child Abuse. (2009). *Commission to inquire into child abuse* (vols. 1–5) (Ryan Report). Stationary Office.

Coulter, C. (1999, July 26). Ombudsman for Children to be appointed to help combat abuse. *The Irish Times*. Available at: https://www.irishtimes.com/news/ombudsman-for-children-to-be-appointed-to-help-combat-abuse-1.210318. Accessed 31 Mar 2021.

Cousins, M. (1996). *Seen and heard: Promoting and protecting children's rights in Ireland*. Children's Rights Alliance.

Dáil Éireann Debate, 21 February 1995, vol. 449, no. 4. Available at: https://www.oireachtas.ie/en/debates/debate/dail/1995-02-21/76/. Accessed 10 Apr 2021.

Dáil Éireann Debate, 4 March 1997, vol. 475, no. 7. Available at: https://www.oireachtas.ie/en/debates/debate/dail/1997-03-04/75/. Accessed 10 Apr 2021.

Dáil Éireann Debate, 24 May 2000, vol. 519, no. 6. Available at: https://www.oireachtas.ie/en/debates/debate/dail/2000-05-24/53/?highlight%5B0%5D=ombudsman&highlight%5B1%5D=bill&highlight%5B2%5D=bill&highlight%5B3%5D=services&highlight%5B4%5D=ombudsman&highlight%5B5%5D=ombudsman&highlight%5B6%5D=ombudsman. Accessed 31 Mar 2021.

Donnelly, S. (2016). Sins of the father: Unravelling moral authority in the Irish Catholic Church. *Irish Journal of Sociology, 24*(3), 315–339.

*The Irish Times*. (2015, June 22). Fr Brendan Smyth: A timeline. *The Irish Times*. Available at: https://www.irishtimes.com/news/crime-and-law/fr-brendan-smyth-a-timeline-1.2258975. Accessed 14 Apr 2021.

Kilkelly, U. (2011). Policing, young people, diversion and accountability in Ireland. *Crime, Law and Social Change, 55*(2–3), 133–151.

Kilkelly, U. (2012). Learning lessons from the past: Legal issues arising from Ireland's child abuse reports. *Irish Journal of Applied Social Studies, 12*(1), article 2, 8–24.

Kilkelly, U. (2015). Children's rights in Ireland: Ireland's relationships with the CRC. In S. Egan (Ed.), *International human rights: Perspectives from Ireland* (pp. 185–199). Bloomsbury Publishing.

Kilkelly, U., & Forde, L. (2021). *Children's rights and police questioning*. The Policing Authority.

Lansdown, G. (2020). National human rights institutions for children. In J. Todres & S. King (Eds.), *The Oxford handbook of children's rights law* (pp. 495–512). Oxford University Press.

Martin, F. (2004). Key roles of the Ombudsman for Children in Ireland: Promotion of rights and investigation of grievances. *Dublin University Law Journal, 26*, 56–82.

McGarry, P. (2019, May 11). Bertie Ahern: State's 1999 apology to abused children was 'absolutely necessary'. *The Irish Times*. Available at: https://www.irishtimes.com/news/social-affairs/religion-and-beliefs/bertie-ahern-state-s-1999-apology-to-abused-children-was-absolutely-necessary-1.3887799. Accessed 31 Mar 2021.

McGuinness, C. (1993). *Kilkenny incest investigation: Report presented to Mr. Brendan Howlin T.D. Minister for Health*. Stationery Office.

Ombudsman Act 1980.

Ombudsman for Children Bill 2002.

Ombudsman for Children Act 2002.

Ombudsman (Amendment) Act 2012.

Ombudsman for Children. (2005). *Annual report 2005*. Ombudsman for Children's Office.

Ombudsman for Children. (2012). *A report by the Ombudsman for Children on the operation of the Ombudsman for Children Act, 2002*. Ombudsman for Children's Office.

Ombudsman for Children. (2013). *Annual report 2013*. Ombudsman for Children's Office.

Ombudsman for Children. (2014). *Annual report 2014*. Ombudsman for Children's Office.

O'Mahony, C., & Kilkelly, U. (2014). O'Keeffe v Ireland and the duty of the state to identify and prevent child abuse. *Journal of Social Welfare and Family Law, 36*(3), 320–329.

O'Morain, P. (1998, January 8). Child group wants ombudsman promise carried through. *The Irish Times*. Available at: https://www.irishtimes.com/news/child-group-wants-ombudsman-promise-carried-through-1.122007. Accessed 14 Apr 2021.

Raftery, M. (1999). *States of Fear*. RTE Television, 24 April, 4 May, 11 May.

RTE. (1999, May 11). *Taoiseach apologies to victims of child abuse*. Available at: https://www.rte.ie/news/1999/0511/1662-abuse/. Accessed 31 Mar 2021.

Seanad Éireann Debate, *Ombudsman for Children Bill, 2002: Second Stage*, 21 February 2002, vol. 169, no. 7. Available at: https://www.oireachtas.ie/en/debates/debate/seanad/2002-02-21/6/. Accessed 12 Apr 2021.

Seanad Éireann Debate, 25 April 2002, vol. 169, no. 22. Available at: https://www.oireachtas.ie/en/debates/debate/seanad/2002-04-25/3/. Accessed 31 Mar 2021.

Smyth, P. (1998, January 13). O'Donnell questioned by UN group for six hours. *The Irish Times*. Available at: https://www.irishtimes.com/news/o-donnell-questioned-by-un-group-for-six-hours-1.123630. Accessed 31 Mar 2021.

UN Convention on the Rights of the Child (CRC). 1989.

UN Committee on the Rights of the Child. (1996). *State Party Report: Ireland*, 17 June 1996, CRC/C/11/Add.12.

UN Committee on the Rights of the Child. (1998). *Concluding Observations: Ireland*, 4 February 1998, CRC/C/15/Add.85.

UN Committee on the Rights of the Child. (2002, November 15). *General Comment No. 2 (2002): The role of independent national human rights institutions in the promotion and protection of the rights of the child*, CRC/GC/2002/2.

UN General Assembly. (1993). Principles relating to the status of national institutions (Paris Principles). UN Doc. A/RES/48/134.

CHAPTER 4

# Raising Awareness

**Abstract** The international standards on national human rights institutions (NHRIs) for children prescribe them to have responsibilities for the protection and the promotion of children's rights. In Irish law, the Ombudsman for Children has a duty to promote the rights and welfare of children, including promoting awareness among the public about children's rights, highlighting issues relating to the rights and welfare of children that are of concern to children, and establishing structures to enable the institution to consult with children to fulfil its functions. The different approaches used to promote children's rights are an illustration of the soft power that NHRIs for children can deploy as part of their role. The Ombudsman for Children has promoted children's rights in various ways, in particular using a national awareness campaign that constituted the largest child participation project undertaken in Ireland. The three-part methodology was important to the breadth and credibility of the initiative and helped it to ensure the strategic positioning of the Ombudsman, giving it early national profile and highlighting the importance of the right of children to be heard in decision-making. The limitations of the exercise are viewed against contemporary approaches to consulting with children.

**Keywords** Awareness campaign · Soft power · Child participation · Human rights education · Research





U. Kilkelly and E. Logan, *National Independent Human Rights Institutions for Children*,
https://doi.org/10.1007/978-3-030-80275-2_4

## 4.1 Introduction

In line with international standards on national human rights institutions (NHRIs) for children, the Ombudsman for Children has a duty to promote the rights and welfare of children, including promoting awareness among the public about children's rights, highlighting issues relating to the rights and welfare of children that are of concern to children, and establishing structures to enable consultation with children to fulfil its functions. The different approaches and powers used to promote children's rights are an illustration of the soft power that NHRIs for children can deploy as part of their role.

In its General Comment No. 5, the Committee on the Rights of the Child (the CRC Committee) recognised that individuals need to know what their rights are, which is especially important when traditionally in most, if not all societies, children have not been regarded as rights holders (2003, para. 66). The Committee explains that if the adults around children do not understand the implications of the Convention, and its confirmation of the equal status of children as subjects of rights, then it is unlikely that the rights set out in the Convention will be realised for many children (2003, para. 66).

Against this backdrop, this chapter includes some examples of promotional activities developed by the Ombudsman for Children, featuring in particular a national awareness campaign that constituted the largest ever child participation project in Ireland. In documenting the approach taken, it examines some of the unanticipated difficulties encountered by the institution in the process, while illustrating the role that the project played in the institution's early strategic positioning and planning for its future development. In addition, the chapter identifies the impact of this work on the national profile afforded to the right of children to be heard in decision-making, which ultimately gave expression in national policy through the adoption of the first National Strategy on Children and Young People's Participation in Decision-Making (Department of Children and Youth Affairs, 2015). It reflects on the limitations of the exercise and questions what form an equivalent exercise would take in light of contemporary approaches to consulting with children.

## 4.2 Powers to Promote Children's Rights

In General Comment No. 2, the CRC Committee highlights that the essential purpose of the promotional role of an NHRI for children is to achieve the mainstreaming of children's rights (2002, para. 7) through human rights education which specifically focuses on children in addition to promoting public understanding (2002, para. 19(o)). The Committee outlines specific activities that are directly relevant to the promotion of children's rights. These include: ensuring the views of children are expressed and heard on matters concerning them, promoting the public understanding and awareness of the importance of children's rights, working closely with the media and undertaking or sponsoring research and educational activities in the field, sensitising the Government, public agencies and the general public to the Convention on the Rights of the Child. It also includes undertaking human rights education which specifically focuses on children (CRC Committee, 2002, para. 19). The importance of these functions in the advancement of children's rights and the implementation of the Convention on the Rights of the Child cannot be underestimated (Sedletzki, 2012, p. 5).

The combination of soft power and independence is in the founding legislation of the Ombudsman for Children which sets out the duty to promote the rights and welfare of children. In its first Strategy, the Ombudsman for Children identified a number of priorities in this regard: influencing law, policy and practice; maximising participation and involvement of children and young people in the work of the institution; and building support for children's rights in order to change attitudes (Ombudsman for Children [OCO], 2007a). Over the years, these functions have taken a number of approaches and forms, including interaction with two arms of the state, the parliament as legislators to influence law and policy, and the executive to influence the drafting of primary and secondary legislation (see Chapter 5). The institution has also been proactive in using strategic communications, through media, to regularly inform the public about its work (see for example, Holland, 2004; The Irish Times, 2014). While there was always keen interest from the media in investigations, as illustrated in Chapter 6, at key moments the Ombudsman for Children published opinion pieces to comment on more challenging matters such as when political or public opinion was divided. On these occasions, the institutional independence was of significant value, as was the credibility of the institution being recognised as an independent voice for children. This standing enabled the Ombudsman to speak out about sensitive and controversial matters, when others might have found this difficult. For instance, in 2010 following the publication of a UNICEF report on inter-country adoption in Vietnam, the Irish government suspended negotiations on a new bilateral inter-country adoption agreement (Dáil Éireann Debate, 2010). Adoptive parents were reportedly devastated by the decision (The Clare Champion, 2010). Ahead of the Adoption Authority going to Vietnam to renegotiate a new bilateral agreement, the Ombudsman for Children published an opinion piece on the matter, designed to advise why the best interests of children and children's rights should inform any agreement on the matter (Logan, 2011).

More generally, and in addition to the advisory activity of the Ombudsman for Children considered in Chapter 5, significant efforts were made to generate public and political interest in the publication of the Ombudsman for Children's submissions to the UN Committee on the Rights of the Child by holding public events, covered by print and broadcast media. Indeed, the experience of Ireland's Ombudsman for Children has been that in promoting public understanding and awareness of the importance of children's rights, the value and effectiveness of working closely with the media cannot be overstated.

At the same time, and as explicitly recognised in General Comment No. 2 (CRC Committee, 2002, para. 16), promoting respect for children's rights is inextricably linked with efforts to promote respect for their views as articulated in Article 12 of the Convention on the Rights of the Child (CRC, 1989). Accessibility to and involvement of children is almost exclusively provided for in the mandates of stand-alone institutions, and those in high-income countries have developed this activity to a much greater extent than institutions elsewhere (Sedletzki, 2012). This was certainly the experience of the Irish Ombudsman for Children and to illustrate this, this chapter next presents a unique case study on running a national awareness campaign—the largest child participation project in

Ireland at the time. To appreciate the context for this project, the relevant preparatory work undertaken by the institution and external agencies will first be outlined, along with the approach to the planning and implementation of the national awareness campaign, followed of course by the results.

## 4.3 Participation of Children

In line with the legislation, direct engagement with and participation of children is a central pillar of the work of the Ombudsman for Children in Ireland (OCO, 2019, p. 14). In the earlier part of the institution's development, this included participation of children in the recruitment of the post holder, the establishment of a Youth Advisory Panel, and direct consultation with children on key thematic areas to hear first-hand about their experiences. The extensive and direct engagement of the Ombudsman with Children is documented throughout each annual report, and as the institution has developed and financial and human resources increased from the original budget of €282,000 (OCO, 2005, p. 6) to €2.747 m (OCO, 2019, p. 72), the institution has undertaken a much greater level of in- and outreach work with children, including with children living in institutional environments (OCO, 2019). These initiatives take different forms depending on the issue. For instance, in 2011, the Office undertook two important consultations with children, making recommendations to policymakers for reform based on children's experiences. The first consultation heard from children with experience of homelessness and accessing crisis out-of-hours services while the second heard from approximately 200 children about their experiences of bullying (OCO, 2011). More recently, the Ombudsman engaged with children in direct provision, the asylum accommodation system, to hear about their lived experiences in their accommodation, school, local community and wider society (OCO, 2020). This study played an important role in raising awareness about the inhumane nature of the direct provision system and its impact on children's rights in particular, ultimately leading to a Government commitment to bring it to an end (Kelly, 2020).

### 4.3.1 *The Participation Lab*

In its first year of operation, the Ombudsman established a 'participation lab' (OCO, 2006, p. 22), a concept stimulated by an early strategic decision to meet the institution's obligations under the 2002 Act (s. 7) to promote the rights and welfare of children, including to children themselves. The ratification of the CRC in 1992 had prompted the development of human rights education in Ireland (Irish Human Rights Commission, 2011, pp. 74–75), supported by international programmes such as the UN Decade for Human Rights Education (Irish Human Rights Commission, 2011, pp. 74–75) which in turn informed the development of specific human rights education in primary and secondary level schools from 1995 (Irish Human Rights Commission, 2011, pp. 10–11). Increased recognition of children's rights to participate in decision-making followed, with the publication in 2000 of the first National Children's Strategy (National Children's Office, 2000) whose first Goal was that children would have a voice. To implement that Goal, structures were established to support active citizenship for children, including Dáil na nÓg (youth parliament), Dáil na bPáistí (children's parliament), Comhairle na nÓg (youth councils at local government level) and Comhairle na bPáistí (children's councils at local government level) (see https://www.comhairlenanog.ie/). Around this time, an all-island education programme—Lift Off Initiative—aimed to promote a human rights culture in schools in Ireland, North and South (Irish Human Rights Commission, 2011, p. 13). Although the Ombudsman for Children sought to refine and replicate the success of this programme, with a focus on the direct education of children about their rights, while also engaging schools and teachers, the cost of running a national programme on an outreach basis was considered prohibitive. On the basis that class visits to out-of-school settings could be learning opportunities for exploration and discovery (DeWitt & Storksdieck, 2008), it was decided that the 'participation labs' would instead take place as an 'in-reach' programme in the Ombudsman for Children. A more economical way to run the labs was to pay for a 'tour bus' for each participating school to bring children from all corners of the country to the capital city, Dublin, where the Ombudsman for Children was based, thereby broadening out the potential for participation, especially among schools from areas of least advantage.

The lab was an early iteration of the education programme designed to inform and educate children and young people about the rights of the UN Convention on the Rights of the Child and about the work of the Ombudsman for Children (OCO, 2006, p. 22). It was piloted from September 2006 to December 2006 with ten groups of children and young people from primary and secondary schools and youth projects from a variety of locations taking part in the pilot (OCO, 2006, p. 23). Following its evaluation, the full programme of workshops began in 2007 (OCO, 2006, p. 23).

The lab has since evolved into a much more structured series of education 'Workshops and Seminars' that are facilitated by staff at the Ombudsman for Children (see https://www.oco.ie/childrens-rights/workshops-and-seminars/). Now, every year, hundreds of children with their schools and non-school settings, like youth groups, take part in children's rights education workshops (OCO, 2019). The workshops are intended to complement the human rights education curricula already in use in schools and outside of school, in youth settings (OCO, 2006, p. 22). Children and young people were actively involved in the design of the workshops (OCO, 2006, p. 22). As a result, the focus of the workshops is on making rights real for children and young people by making connections between rights and their daily lives, in an age-appropriate, interactive and fun way. Other developments of the programme include an extension of the workshop back into schools, where visiting children, young people and adults are given a resource pack to encourage them to take action when they return to school or youth project, to raise awareness amongst their peers of children's rights. Some children have taken to writing in school newsletters, on social media or ultimately undertaking bigger projects about children's rights in Ireland. For children and young people who cannot attend, a separate website is available with up-to-date information and resource packs for educators that support children's rights education on an ongoing basis (see https://www.oco.ie/itsyourright/).

## 4.4 The 'Big Ballot'

In the 2006 Annual Report to the Oireachtas (Parliament), the Ombudsman for Children outlined a plan for a project designed to facilitate children in the development of the work priorities of the Ombudsman for Children relevant to the first strategic plan, from 2007 to 2010 and beyond (OCO, 2006, p. 23). However, to undertake such a significant project on a national level required a credible foundation and children's rights framework and this, it was agreed, would be achieved through the commissioning of academic research (OCO, 2007b). The project was to have three individual, but closely linked phases: academic research, a qualitative study involving children and young people, and the holding of a nationwide vote called the 'Big Ballot' in which children and young people would vote on the issues of greatest importance to them (OCO, 2007b, p. 33). Importantly, all three elements had their basis in the Ombudsman's statutory powers, namely the power to undertake, promote or publish research on children's rights; to collect and disseminate information on matters relating to the rights and welfare of children; to highlight issues relating to children's rights that are of concern; and to promote awareness among members of the public, including children, on the principles and provisions of the CRC and how those rights can be enforced (Ombudsman for Children Act, 2002, s. 7).

### *4.4.1 Phase 1: The Academic Research*

To be consistent with the powers of the Ombudsman, and consistent with good practice in other jurisdictions (Kilkelly et al., 2005), it was agreed that the 'Big Ballot' should have a firm academic base. In planning this phase, it was decided to go beyond the study of the areas where children's CRC rights were violated or undermined in Ireland, broadening out the analysis to identify the principal obstacles that prevent children from realising their rights (OCO, 2007b, p. 33). The research sought first to measure the treatment of children in Irish law policy and practice against the CRC (Kilkelly, 2007, p. 13), including the guidance of the Committee on the Rights of the Child, in order to identify the benchmarks against which children's rights were being ignored and where barriers to the realisation of those rights existed (Kilkelly & Lundy, 2006). Thematic areas were developed based on the reporting guidelines of the CRC Committee (CRC Committee, 1991) including the following headings: family, environment and alternative care; health, wealth and material deprivation; education; play, leisure and recreation; and youth justice. In addition, two cross-cutting themes were used—children and young people's right to be heard and vulnerable children, including children needing special protection with a view to promoting greater breadth across the study in these important areas (Kilkelly, 2007).

The research provided the basis for a resource tool allowing for the design and operation of the qualitative research study. The findings indicated in some detail that, in Ireland, children faced multiple problems in the realisation of their rights with certain children—such as children in the care and justice systems, Traveller children, children living in poverty, and asylum seeking children—facing multiple barriers in this regard (Kilkelly, 2007, p. 169). Six barriers to the implementation of children's rights were identified as: the invisibility of children in decision-making structures; the absence of children's rights from law and policy; the inadequacy of mechanisms for complaints, monitoring and advocacy; the inadequacy of supports and services; the absence of investment; and the need for greater information and training (Kilkelly, 2007, p. 61).

This research served three main purposes. First, it assisted in identifying the principal obstacles to the implementation of children's rights in Ireland, highlighting the strategic direction for the Ombudsman for Children, including research and policy programmes designed to overcome the obstacles in question (OCO, 2006, p. 12). Second, the research established a baseline against which to measure future progress (OCO, 2006, p. 13) and third, the research provided the framework for the 'voice' or third phase of the project, which would facilitate the participation of children in the development of priority areas of work for the Ombudsman for Children (OCO, 2006, p. 13).

### 4.4.2 *Phase 2: Testing the Findings of the Academic Research with Children*

Building on the phase one 'Barriers' study, the second phase of the project involved consultation with 150 children from all parts of the country, and from representative backgrounds, sought to test its findings (OCO, 2007b, 2007c). In these sessions, the children examined, discussed and explored the obstacles presented in the research and translated them into a list of five issues they perceived as most relevant to their own lives (OCO, 2007b, p. 33).

The issues, which all relate to rights listed in the UN Convention on the Rights of the Child, were as follows:

1. Education;
2. Play and Recreation;
3. Having a Voice;

4. Family and Care;
5. Health, wealth and material well-being (OCO, 2007b, p. 34).

The second phase thus built on the first phase of the project by providing feedback from the children involved about issues of importance to them and the obstacles they faced in realising their rights (Kilkelly, 2007, pp. 15–16).

### 4.4.3 *Phase 3: The Vote*

The planning for phase three of the project (the 'Big Ballot', so-called because it was due to take place the same year as a General Election) began long before the publication of the 'Barriers' research (OCO, 2006, p. 23). The first task was to establish a steering group for the project and in addition to identifying key staff with appropriate skills within the office of the Ombudsman for Children, the support of an external expert was enlisted. The well-respected Director of Advocacy from Barnardos (see https://www.barnardos.ie), a large and influential children's NGO in Ireland, joined the steering group and her expertise and support was to prove extremely beneficial as the project progressed and she played the role of critical friend bringing objective oversight to the project.

The next task was to build national support for the project. As the participation of children was going to take place in and through schools, the Ombudsman for Children began building support for the project through extensive consultation with key education stakeholders. Taken together, the three teachers' trade unions in Ireland have numerical strength and have increasing influence on educational policy (Drudy, 2001). It was highly significant then that all three such organisations—the Irish National Teachers' Organisation, the Association of Secondary Teachers of Ireland and the Teachers' Union of Ireland—agreed to support the project.

It was equally important to consider children and young people outside of the mainstream school system such as early school leavers, children from the Traveller community who may not attend school and children being home-schooled. The Ombudsman for Children sought the support of Youthreach, a national education programme that works with early school leavers to provide a tailored approach to education geared to the specific needs of individual young people (see http://cityofdublin.etb.ie/youthreach/). In addition, the Ombudsman for Children sought support from Senior Traveller Training Centres, which at that time provided basic compensatory education for Travellers, including young Travellers between the ages of 15 and 18 (Foley, 2008; OCO, 2010, p. 2). Both Youthreach leaders and Senior Traveller Training centres offered their support to the project (OCO, 2010, p. 2) along with other organisations, including professional networks, and parent organisations like the National Parents Council (see https://www.npc.ie).

In order to assist teachers in preparing children to participate in the Big Ballot, the assistance and advice of the national co-ordinator for civic, social and political education in schools was enlisted. The staff of the Ombudsman for Children worked with two teams of experienced resource writers to produce teacher-friendly and age-appropriate resource materials, including materials on each of the five thematic areas identified by children and young people in the qualitative research study in phase two (OCO, 2007b, p. 34). These materials complemented the school resources, helping to embed children's rights into the national school curriculum.

Finally, on the basis that this was going to be the largest ever national consultation with children, the Ombudsman for Children met with the Head of Children's Content at Ireland's national television broadcaster, RTE, to explain the project, its purpose and methodology. This collaboration also aimed to seek support for television coverage of the campaign in order to promote the participation of as many schools as possible and to ensure that the final element of the project, the children and young people's vote, due to take place over a week in November that year, was a success. With media support secured, the Ombudsman for Children, staff and members of the Youth Advisory Panel, over a period of a month, travelled the country in a specially branded 'Big Ballot' bus to visit schools and education centres (OCO, 2007b, pp. 33–34). The tour, which allowed the Ombudsman to meet approximately five thousand children and dozens of teachers, principals and youth workers, was also an opportunity to support, encourage and show appreciation to everyone for their willingness to be involved in the project (OCO, 2007b, p. 34). The initiative received strong media profile, with a television camera and reporter turning up to a number of schools around the country to cover the progress of the Big Ballot, with the news reaching hundreds of thousands of homes (RTE, 2007). The project culminated in a referendum style vote, designed to take place over the course of one week so that the schools had time to work out the logistics. As the vote was to mirror some of the elements of a general election, with polling stations, count centres and returning officers situated in participating schools, logistics were an important consideration.

What happened next was unexpected. A father of six children made an ex parte application to the High Court seeking leave to judicially review the authority of the Ombudsman for Children to conduct the Big Ballot and seeking an injunction to stop the event going ahead. The lay litigant claimed that the Ombudsman for Children had exceeded her statutory powers in asking the schools to undertake the project, which he argued 'undermined the rights of parents', was an 'impermissible attack on the authority of the family' and was 'likely to lead to an undermining of social order and to harm the educational welfare of the children involved' (Carolan, 2007). However, the judge ruled that the applicant did not have the required legal standing to challenge the Ombudsman for Children's actions and had failed to establish an arguable case (Carolan, 2007).

In finding against the applicant, the judge remarked that while the project sought to highlight and raise awareness among children of their rights, he found it 'curious' that there was 'so little mention' of the constitutional and legal protections afforded to the family (Carolan, 2007). He noted that under the Education Act 1998 parents were entitled to exempt their children from participating (Carolan, 2007), a measure designed to provide reassurance that an appropriate balance had been struck in the circumstances. Although the legal challenge failed, it was an important reminder of the strength of the constitutional standing enjoyed by parents and the availability of legal remedies to those seeking to prevent what could be argued to be an illegitimate interference with that authority.

Following this dramatic but temporary interruption of the project, the vote went ahead as planned over the course of the week in November 2007. In excess of 74,000 children and young people in 560 schools around the country voted in the Big Ballot, the largest consultation with children and young people ever held in Ireland (OCO, 2007b, pp. 33–34), and the results were announced at a special count event, compered by a national television presenter and regular anchor for general elections, bringing both excitement and gravitas to the day (RTE, 2007). The event took place in Dublin on 20 November, Universal Children's Day (OCO, 2007b, p. 34), and 500 children and young people travelled to the 'count centre' to hear the results. The event was a large-scale public occasion, covered by multiple media sources, which allowed the Ombudsman for

Children not only to respond to the results but also to thank everyone for the huge support received from a wide range of education stakeholders and from schools who worked hard to ensure their students participated, and who made the Big Ballot such a success (OCO, 2007b, pp. 33–35).

The results of the 74,000 votes on the rights that mattered most to children were as follows:

1. Family and Care—31.5%
2. Play and Recreation—24%
3. Having a Voice—16.5%
4. Health, Wealth and Material Wellbeing—16%
5. Education—12%.

At the outset, a system of feedback from interested educators to the Ombudsman for Children's institution was established on an ongoing basis. Feedback on the project indicated that the principal, perceived benefits of the participation of children included the opportunity to explore children's rights; to form and express opinions; and to learn about taking part in a democratic process (OCO, 2010, p. 2). Generally, teachers spoke very positively about their experience of using the resource materials provided by the Ombudsman for Children's institution for the Big Ballot project and sought further materials on children's rights from the institution (OCO, 2010, p. 2). In addition to emails, the Ombudsman for Children received over one hundred letters from children themselves about the experience, with both teachers and children expressing enthusiasm for the project and making recommendations about how future projects could be improved.

Following the conclusion of the Big Ballot project, education materials were further developed including lesson plans and activities for educators working with children and young people (see https://www.oco.ie/childrens-rights/education-materials/). By 2010, such a significant amount of material had been generated by schools and children themselves that a separate website to host information for children and parents about children's rights was developed (see https://www.oco.ie/itsyourright). This also included videos for more creative contributions (see https://www.youtube.com/user/OCOIreland) and more recently, the resource materials include interactive games where children can engage in learning about their rights (see https://www.oco.ie/itsyourright/

game/), by different age groups (see https://www.oco.ie/itsyourright/13-plus-years-old/).

### 4.4.4 *Reflections on the Big Ballot*

Although no formal evaluation of the Big Ballot project was undertaken, reflections on the project over time have revealed the pros and cons of the approach taken. In general, it is evident that the three-part methodology gave breadth and credibility to the initiative and helped it to ensure the strategic positioning of the Ombudsman at an early stage in the life of the institution. It also highlighted, with depth and reach, the national profile of the office and showed the importance of ensuring that children are heard in decision-making, on this occasion feeding directly into the strategy of the Ombudsman for Children. It also served to embed consultation with children into the practice of the office early in its development.

The project announced the arrival of the Ombudsman for Children in Ireland. As a new institution, it was important to do this with a national initiative that sought to reach a wide range and number of children from different backgrounds, informing them about their rights, engaging them in dialogue and prompting them to reflect on what rights mattered most to them. The key rights themes were generated through desk-based academic research and the credibility of the process was further enhanced by testing the priorities against the views of a very large group of children before being put to thousands nationally. The nature of the exercise—that required children to place the rights in rank order—meant that the Big Ballot was associated with learning not just about children's rights but also about the democratic process. The situation of a large-scale children's rights awareness raising project in the educational domain was consistent with the international standards—including Article 42 and Article 29 of the CRC—and this helped to emphasise the importance of human rights education for children. It also gave the project structure, prompting school ownership of the initiative in a way that gave it both longevity and sustainability. The enduring nature of the resources is testament to that. In addition to making a connection between the new institution and children themselves, the Big Ballot connected the institution to its other stakeholders—teachers, civil society organisations and the media for instance—in line with the international standards and these were relationships that were to prove more important as the role of the Ombudsman evolved. In addition, the project had the effect of positioning the Office at the centre of the child's right to be involved in decision-making nationally (Sinclair, 2004), and as an early national initiative of its kind, it offered support to the adoption of the first National Strategy on the participation of children and young people in decision-making (Department of Children and Youth Affairs, 2015). It also had an impact internationally in that it was replicated in at least one other jurisdiction (Scotland's Commissioner for Children and Young People, 2012).

In terms of lessons learned, it is clear that the project was an enormous logistical challenge, demanding resources and capacity that extended beyond the Ombudsman's small team at the time. Schools' preference for hard copies of materials meant that the administration of the project was very demanding, while its interruption by a legal challenge involved stress of another kind, even if that was unsuccessful. Significantly, although the inclusion of the Constitution in the materials might have offset the risk of any legal challenge, a strategic decision was made not to do so as it could have distracted from the more universal and accessible message of the Convention. Although its success can only be measured by engaging directly with the children who participated, from the Ombudsman's perspective, the project achieved the goals set out—bringing the new institution into the lives of Ireland's children, increasing awareness about their rights and creating space for dialogue and understanding about what children's rights mean to them. Evident limitations were largely those related to resources, prompting consideration of whether ambition in this domain should be tempered by pragmatism. What is clear, however, is that in the future, any such initiative would have to be led by the children themselves and in the digital age, it is likely that a very different approach would be taken deploying the tools of social media and technology.

## 4.5 Conclusion

The Committee on the Rights of the Child has recognised the important role of NHRIs for children in the implementation of the Convention, including a combination of activities designed to protect and promote children's rights (2002, para. 19). The listing of these measures—to raise awareness among and to listen to children about their rights—suggests perhaps that these are distinct activities, their potential for influence categorised as 'soft power'. As this chapter illustrates, the experience of the Ombudsman for Children has been that to view the promotional role of an NHRI for children as less important than monitoring is to ignore its transformative potential. Certainly, the Irish experience is that not only can such initiatives be effective in raising awareness about children's rights, but they can also serve to raise the profile of the organisation itself, enhancing the public and political confidence in the institution, augmenting the credibility and integrity of its work in other areas.

A recent study of child participation research found a remarkably consistent narrative over the 30-year life of the CRC, that there was much more written about challenges than solutions (McMellon & Tisdall, 2020). The aim of this chapter was to address this apparent shortfall by illustrating what form an exercise in national child participation can take, in the life of a newly formed national human rights institution for children. While a similar initiative would take a very different form in 2021—with the online domain replacing the bus as the vehicle for delivering children information about their rights perhaps—ensuring the multi-dimensional purpose and nature of the exercise would require considerable thought and creativity. While adults lament the dangers of social media, its democratisation of information has provided opportunities for children to mobilise in ways never before conceived. Children are now leading not only local campaigns but global campaigns—like the Fridays for Future for climate justice and the National School Walkouts on gun violence. One question remains: if the Big Ballot were to take place today, how different might it look?

## References

Barnardos. https://www.barnardos.ie. Accessed 8 Apr 2021.

Carolan, M. (2007, November 10). Challenge to children's ballot fails. *The Irish Times*. Available at: https://www.irishtimes.com/news/challenge-to-children-s-ballot-fails-1.980776. Accessed 7 Apr 2021.

City of Dublin Education and Training Board, Youthreach. http://cityofdublin.etb.ie/youthreach/. Accessed 8 Apr 2021.

Comhairle na nÓg. https://www.comhairlenanog.ie/. Accessed 10 Apr 2021.

Dáil Éireann Debate. (2010, June 15). *Inter-country adoptions*. Available at: https://www.oireachtas.ie/en/debates/question/2010-06-15/159/. Accessed 7 Apr 2021.

Department of Children and Youth Affairs. (2015). *National strategy on children and young people's participation in decision-making, 2015–2020*. Government Publications. Available at: www.dcya.ie. Accessed 12 Apr 2021.

DeWitt, J., & Storksdieck, M. (2008). A short review of school field trips: Key findings from the past and implications for the future. *Visitor Studies, 11*(2), 181–197.

Drudy, S. (2001). The teaching profession in Ireland: Its role and current challenges. *Studies: An Irish Quarterly Review, 90*(360), 363–375.

Foley, M. (2008). *An evaluation of the role of senior traveller training centres*. Masters Dissertation. DIT. Available at: https://arrow.tudublin.ie/aaschssldis/23/. Accessed 12 Apr 2021.

Holland, K. (2004, June 3). Ombudsman for Children concerned about referendum. *The Irish Times*. Available at: https://www.irishtimes.com/news/ombudsman-for-children-concerned-about-referendum-1.1143186. Accessed 6 Apr 2021.

Irish Human Rights Commission. (2011). *Human rights education in Ireland: An overview*. Irish Human Rights Commission.

Kelly, F. (2020, June 14). Direct provision system to be ended within life of next government. *The Irish Times*. Available at: https://www.irishtimes.com/news/politics/direct-provision-system-to-be-ended-within-life-of-next-government-1.4278954?mode=sample&auth-failed=1&pw-origin=https%3A%2F%2Fwww.irishtimes.com%2Fnews%2Fpolitics%2Fdirect-provision-system-to-be-ended-within-life-of-next-government-1.4278954. Accessed 6 Apr 2021.

Kilkelly, U. (2007). *Barriers to the realisation of children's rights in Ireland*. Ombudsman for Children's Office.

Kilkelly, U., Kilpatrick, R., Lundy, L. et al. (2005) *Children's rights in Ireland*. Northern Ireland Commissioner for Children and Young People.

Kilkelly, U., & Lundy, L. (2006). Children's rights in action: Using the UN Convention on the Rights of the Child as an auditing tool. *Child and Family Law Quarterly, 18*(3), 331–350.

Logan, E. (2011, April 18). Rights of children key issue in applying best practice to inter-country adoption. *The Irish Times*. Available at: https://www.irishtimes.com/search/archive.html?q=adoption&fromDate=18%2F04%2F2011&toDate=18%2F04%2F2011&rm=listresults&filter=. Accessed 6 Apr 2021.

McMellon, C., & Tisdall, E. K. M. (2020). Children and young people's participation rights: Looking backwards and moving forwards. *The International Journal of Children's Rights, 28*(1), 157–182.

National Children's Office. (2000). *National children's strategy: Our children—Their lives*. Stationery Office.

National Parents Council. https://www.npc.ie. Accessed 8 Apr 2021.

Ombudsman for Children Act 2002.

Ombudsman for Children. (2005). *Annual report 2005*. Ombudsman for Children's Office.

Ombudsman for Children. (2006). *Respecting children: Annual report of the Ombudsman for Children's office April 2005–December 2006*. Ombudsman for Children's Office.

Ombudsman for Children. (2007a). *Strategic plan 2007–2010*. Ombudsman for Children's Office. Available at: https://www.oco.ie/app/uploads/2010/05/OCOStrategicPlan07-10.pdf. Accessed 6 Apr 2021.

Ombudsman for Children. (2007b). *Hearing children: Annual report of the Ombudsman for Children's office January 2007–December 2007*. Ombudsman for Children's Office.

Ombudsman for Children. (2007c). Over 1000 schools & education centres to take part in the OCO's Big Ballot, Press Release. Available at: https://www.oco.ie/news/1000-schools-education-centres-take-part-ocos-big-ballot/. Accessed 6 Apr 2021.

Ombudsman for Children. (2010). *What do you say? Exploring children's rights and understanding what the Ombudsman for Children does*. Ombudsman for Children's Office. Available at: https://www.oco.ie/childrens-rights/education-materials/. Accessed 10 Apr 2021.

Ombudsman for Children. (2011). *Annual report 2011*. Ombudsman for Children's Office.

Ombudsman for Children. (2019). *Progress for children: Annual report 2019*. Ombudsman for Children's Office.

Ombudsman for Children. (2020). *Direct division: Children's views and experiences of living in direct provision. A report by the Ombudsman for Children's Office 2020*. Ombudsman for Children's Office.

Ombudsman for Children's Office, 'It's your right'. https://www.oco.ie/itsyourright. Accessed 6 Apr 2021.

Ombudsman for Children's Office, 'It's your right game'. https://www.oco.ie/itsyourright/game/. Accessed 8 Apr 2021.

Ombudsman for Children's Office, '13+ years old', https://www.oco.ie/itsyourright/13-plus-years-old/. Accessed 8 Apr 2021.

Ombudsman for Children's Office, Lesson plans and activities for those working with children and young people. Available at: https://www.oco.ie/childrens-rights/education-materials/. Accessed 6 Apr 2021.

Ombudsman for Children's Office, Workshops and Seminars. Available at: https://www.oco.ie/childrens-rights/workshops-and-seminars/. Accessed 6 Apr 2021.

OCOIreland YouTube channel. https://www.youtube.com/user/OCOIreland. Accessed 8 Apr 2021.

RTE. (2007, November 20). *The big ballot—Children have their say*. Available at: https://www.rte.ie/news/special-reports/2007/1120/96190-bigballot/. Accessed 6 Apr 2021.

Scotland's Commissioner for Children and Young People. (2012). *A Right wee blether*. Scotland's Commissioner for Children and Young People.
Sedletzki, V. (2012). *Championing Children's Rights: A global study of independent human rights institutions for children—Summary report*. Innocenti Publications.
Sinclair, R. (2004). Participation in practice: Making it meaningful, effective and sustainable. *Children & Society, 18*(2), 106–118.
The Clare Champion. (2010, January 21). Adoptive parents devastated by Vietnam decision. *The Clare Champion*. Available at: https://clarechampion.ie/adoptive-parents-devastated-by-vietnam-decision/. Accessed 6 Apr 2021.
The Irish Times. (2014). Ombudsman for Children. *The Irish Times*. Available at: https://www.irishtimes.com/sponsored/ombudsman-for-children. Accessed 6 Apr 2021.
United Nations Convention on the Rights of the Child (CRC) 1989.
UN Committee on the Rights of the Child. (1991). General guidelines regarding the form and content of initial reports to be submitted by States parties under article 44, paragraph 1 (a), of the Convention: Convention on the Rights of the Child / adopted by the Committee at its 22nd meeting (1st session) on 15 October 1991, 30 October 1991, CRC/C/5. UN
UN Committee on the Rights of the Child. (2002). *General Comment No. 2 (2002): The Role of Independent National Human Rights Institutions in the Promotion and Protection of the Rights of the Child*, 15 November 2002, CRC/GC/2002/2.
UN Committee on the Rights of the Child. (2003). *General Comment No. 5 (2003): General measures of implementation of the Convention on the Rights of the Child*, 27 November 2003, CRC/GC/2003/5.

CHAPTER 5

# Advising Government

**Abstract** A key role for any national human rights institution (NHRI) for children is to provide guidance and advice to Government on the harmonisation of law and policy with children's rights. In line with international standards, the Ombudsman for Children has a mandate to make submissions on proposed, draft or operating legislation from a children's rights perspective. In this regard, the Ombudsman for Children has commented, advised and made submissions on a variety of legislative proposals, ranging from child protection to education, from sexual offences to adoption. This work has been thematic at times—drawing pieces of legislation together—while it has also drawn on the experience of other aspects of the role, specifically the complaint function. There are a number of benefits to this work, including the opportunity to use the independence and authority of the institution to speak against, as well as in favour of Government proposals. The Ombudsman for Children has been highly active in this area although a more formal evaluation of its impact should be undertaken. Consideration might also be given to advocating for a children's rights impact assessment mechanism to harmonise law and policy with the Convention on the Rights of the Child more systematically.

**Keywords** Advice · Law reform · Accountability · Watchdog · Children's rights · Parliament



U. Kilkelly and E. Logan, *National Independent Human Rights Institutions for Children*,
https://doi.org/10.1007/978-3-030-80275-2_5

## 5.1 Introduction

As Chapter 2 explains, one of the key functions of a national human rights institution (NHRI) is to act as an independent source of guidance and advice to Government on human rights matters within its mandate. As the Paris Principles (UN General Assembly, 1993) recognise, it is important to this function that the institution is set up in such a way that enables it to provide such advice, without fear or favour, while having the necessary integrity and standing to be taken seriously in this regard. The Committee on the Rights of the Child (the CRC Committee) has made it clear that NHRIs for children are part of the national infrastructure to support implementation of the Convention on the Rights of the Child (CRC, 1989), making it important both that the institution finds its authority in the Convention, while itself acting in line with the Convention's general principles. It is especially crucial, therefore, that NHRIs for children are inclusive of all children, act in children's best interests at all times and both listen directly to children, appropriately involving and consulting them, while involving children in the establishment, organisation and activities of the institution (CRC Committee, 2002, paras. 15–16). In this respect, the advice and guidance provided by the NHRIs for children must be both rooted in the Convention and informed by the views, experiences and perspectives of children themselves.

According to the CRC Committee, NHRIs must have the right to report 'directly, independently and separately on the state of children's rights to the public and to parliamentary bodies' (CRC Committee, 2002, para. 18). This can include publishing reports and recommendations on any matters relevant to the rights of children of their own volition or at the request of national authorities, keeping the adequacy of law and policy under review from a children's rights perspective. It can also include promoting the harmonisation of law and policy with the Convention through the 'provision of advice to public and private bodies in construing and applying the Convention' (CRC Committee, 2002, para. 19). The Committee also highlights the important role played by NHRIs for children in advocating for and facilitating 'meaningful participation by children's rights NGOs …in the development of domestic legislation and international instruments on issues affecting children' (CRC Committee, 2002, para. 19).

These functions are set out in the Ombudsman for Children Act 2002, which requires the Ombudsman to advise Government on the development and co-ordination of policy relating to children and to 'monitor and review' the operation of legislation concerning matters that relate to the rights and welfare of children (Ombudsman for Children Act, 2002, s. 7). Separately, the Act provides that the Ombudsman may either on their own initiative or on the request of Government give advice on any matter relating to the rights and welfare of children. This specifically includes advice regarding the 'probable effect on children of the implementation of any proposals for legislation' (Ombudsman for Children Act, 2002, s. 7). To a large extent, therefore, the legislation founding the Irish Ombudsman for Children reflects the international standards on the role of the NHRI for children as the provider to Government of impartial advice on children's rights issues and as a trusted, independent source of authoritative guidance on the rights and welfare of children. Over the course of its life, the Ombudsman for Children has fulfilled this function in a number of ways that have addressed different areas of concern from a children's rights perspective. First, as mandated by the legislation (Ombudsman for Children Act, 2002, s. 13), the Ombudsman has issued an Annual Report to the Oireachtas (Parliament) as a key means of ensuring accountability. Second, the Ombudsman has provided advice to Government on draft legislation referred to it for its consideration and has, of its own volition, provided advice on legislative proposals and other matters and third, it has published a number of reports, including to parliamentary committees, on matters relevant to children's rights.

This chapter presents an analysis of this work, providing an overview of the kind of presentations made to Government on legislative matters and analysing the kind of approach taken to this work. Particular consideration is given here to the role played by the Ombudsman for Children in the campaign to amend the Irish Constitution to include children's rights. Taken together, this body of work represents the variety and depth of the proactive and reactive work of the Ombudsman in the promotion and protection of children's rights. It also highlights the important connections that can be drawn between the three different functions of the institution, which is vital if its resources and mandate are to be maximised.

## 5.2 Accountability to Parliament

Under its founding legislation, the Ombudsman for Children is required to present an annual report to Parliament on its work and from the establishment of the Ombudsman in 2004 to date, there have been 15 such reports, detailing the activity and achievements of the institution. The reports provide important benchmarks on the role and reach of the institution, documenting the extent of public engagement and range and depth of issues addressed with and on behalf of children. On the one hand, they stand as an important record of progress in the harmonisation of national law and policy with the Convention, while on the other, they identify the gaps and barriers that continue to frustrate the full implementation of children's rights in Ireland. As a mechanism of accountability, the Reports present to Parliament an important snapshot of the diversity of activity undertaken by the Ombudsman for Children in line with its mandate, including education and promotion activity, submissions to Government in compliance with its monitoring function and the increasing recourse to the complaint function. While the complaint function is explored in more detail in the next chapter, it is worth noting here that the reports present Parliament with detailed statistical data on the complaints received annually against public bodies, a summary of the headings under which these complaints routinely fall and some information on the outcomes achieved for individual children, by case study. The reports thus promote public accountability on behalf of child complainants insofar as they bring to public attention the challenges many children face seeking to have their rights vindicated, and they illuminate in varying ways, the role that public bodies play in that process.

The annual reports illustrate both the depth of work undertaken every year, while they also highlight the integrated nature of the different parts of the Ombudsman's role. They include important commentary on the fulfilment of the Ombudsman's mandate, including information on the limitations placed on the role by insufficient resources (Ombudsman for Children [OCO], 2007a) and staffing (OCO, 2008) and drawing attention to the inadequacies in the legislative mandate (OCO, 2009). In addition to the exclusions in the legislation, explained in Chapter 3, the experience of administering complaints has also helped to reveal other factors that impede the operation of the legislation. For instance, in 2008, the Ombudsman noted that the duty to inform a parent when a complaint is received from a child could be prohibitive when, for instance, the child has made an allegation of abuse against the child's parent (OCO, 2008). The Annual Report also noted the impact on children in care of the fact that complaints cannot be received once the child reaches 18 years—the comparison is made with other jurisdictions where complaints are permitted in certain instances from those up to 21 years (OCO, 2008).

The Reports have also been directed at wider Government, highlighting to all Government departments, not just those with responsibility for legislation, the importance of seeking the independent advice of the Ombudsman on matters relating to children (OCO, 2008). The Ombudsman has also highlighted the need to ensure that advice is sought early in the drafting process if it is to have real effect (OCO, 2010). The Annual Reports also present important perspectives on children's rights issues that should be taken into account in law and policymaking that cuts across the areas of health, education and justice for example (OCO, 2011). Periodically, the reports are used to reflect on progress made—constitutional reform for instance and the ending of the imprisonment of children (OCO, 2013)—while the operation of the Ombudsman for Children Act is a source of regular commentary (OCO, 2018).

Two final themes are important from the Annual Reports and both highlight important powers of the Ombudsman in line with international standards and the national legislation. The first is the importance attached to research. Attention is paid in General Comment No. 2 to the role that research can play in generating awareness about children's rights (CRC Committee, 2002, para. 19) and the 2002 Act (s. 7) specifically provides that the Ombudsman for Children may 'undertake, promote or publish research into any matter relating to the rights and welfare of children'. As a result of both influences, research has underpinned the mandate of the Office since the commissioning of the early study on the Barriers to the Implementation of Children's Rights (Kilkelly, 2007) that informed the Big Ballot project, explained in Chapter 4. It has also been evident in other areas, such as in relation to the participation work of the Office which was originally scoped out by a study completed by the Children's Research Centre in Trinity College Dublin so as to provide 'a solid foundation' for the development of the Office's participation model (OCO, 2006, p. 21). In just these two examples, the credibility and integrity of the Office was strengthened by being underpinned and informed by robust academic research. The importance of using research to strengthen the Ombudsman's role was identified as an early strategic priority of the institution which committed, additionally, to research that was child-centred and human rights-based, action-oriented, and used to strengthen its main functions in an integrated and co-ordinated manner (OCO, 2005a).

The second priority evident from the work of the Ombudsman for Children is the attention paid to international and regional networking. Both the CRC and the Committee's guidance highlight the importance of international and regional co-operation in order to share experience and exchange expertise on the implementation of children's rights (CRC Committee, 2002). This was translated in a specific way into the Ombudsman for Children Act 2002 which requires that the Ombudsman for Children 'exchange information and co-operate with the Ombudsman for Children (by whatever name called) of other states' (s. 7). From the outset, the Annual Reports to Parliament highlight that the Ombudsman for Children has not just been connected regionally and internationally, but early on took up leadership in this sector. Indeed, the international context featured in the very first report of the office (OCO, 2005a) which noted the Irish Ombudsman for Children's membership of the European Network of Ombudspersons for Children (ENOC) , while the 2006 Report noted the hosting by the Ombudsman of the British and Irish Network of Ombudsman and Children's Commissioners (BINOCC) in Dublin that year (OCO, 2006). In 2008, the Ombudsman for Children was elected chair of ENOC, hosting the high-profile international conference of the network (OCO, 2008) and since that time, the international positioning of the Office has continued to be an important part of its identity, with added mutual benefit to institutions in Ireland and overseas. In addition to reporting annually on routine interaction at international level, in June 2008 this formed the basis of a submission to both the Oireachtas Joint Committee on Foreign Affairs and the Joint Committee on European Affairs documenting the Ombudsman's interaction with international networks and organisations working in the field of children's rights (OCO, 2008). Not only has this activity taken place in regional or international networks, it has also involved engagement in a bilateral manner with senior UN office holders such as the UN Special Representative on Violence against Children, the UN High Commissioner on Refugees and the Council of Europe Commissioner for Human Rights. Active membership of a growing international community can only aid the development of the national institution, as knowledge and expertise are shared with regard to children's rights issues and the solidarity of the group is available should any institutions face a national or international challenge. Examples of this are evident throughout this book.

The priority afforded to international engagement is also evident from the routine and meaningful engagement that has taken place between the Ombudsman for Children and international treaty monitoring bodies. In addition to the influential role that the institution has had in Ireland's reports to the Committee under the CRC, the institution has engaged with the Universal Periodic Review process (OCO, 2011, 2021), the Committee for the Prevention of Torture (OCO, 2014), the Special Rapporteur on the sale and sexual exploitation of children (OCO, 2018) and has been cited by the UN Committee against Torture (OCO, 2012).

## 5.3 Guidance and Advice to Government

The Ombudsman for Children has an express duty to provide guidance to Government on proposals for legislative reform, both on request and on their own volition. This process can take different forms depending on the circumstances and the issue, including submissions on early legislative proposals and on draft legislation. In the lifetime of the Ombudsman for Children, many legislative proposals and draft laws have been referred to it for review, while in other situations this advice has been invited following an intervention from the Ombudsman or in other cases, proactively presented. It is important that the Ombudsman for Children Act 2002 has both the discretion and, where requested, the duty to provide advice to Government 'on any matter (including the probable effect on children of the implementation of any proposals for legislation) relating to the rights and welfare of children' (s. 7). Combined with the duty to monitor and review the operation of legislation and to advise Government on the development and co-ordination of policy (Ombudsman for Children Act, 2002, s. 7), these functions have proven to be critically important to the public profile and the political influence of the institution. Government has referred multiple draft laws or legislative proposals to the institution for consideration from a children's rights perspective. These have included legislation concerning youth justice (OCO, 2006), asylum and refugee law (OCO, 2008) and family relationships (OCO, 2014), all of which have an obvious and direct bearing on children's rights. Here, as in other areas, the advice presented sought to strengthen the extent to which the legislation meets international human rights standards. The Ombudsman for Children has also presented observations to Government on legislative proposals with perhaps a less obvious impact on children's rights, such as in the area of spent convictions. This legislation provided for the non-disclosure of criminal records under certain circumstances and after a certain period of time. It specifically excluded employment which would involve contact with children and the Ombudsman for Children's advice was aimed at ensuring these exclusions were sufficiently comprehensive (OCO, 2009). The influence of the Ombudsman's observations has been particularly evident in the numerous submissions made in the area of child protection, including several legislative proposals that addressed sexual offences, safeguarding and human trafficking. In addition to making recommendations that strengthen the children's rights provisions in these laws—such as protecting from the risk of secondary victimisation and ensuring children are treated equally with regard to gender—the contribution of the Ombudsman for Children has served to identify the connections between the different pieces of legislation, highlighting the need for a consistent and integrated approach. In this way, the institution promoted a more coherent approach to the broad area of child protection, in line with children's rights, rather than improving the harmonisation of each individual piece of legislation with the Convention (OCO, 2010).

The sustained focus of the institution on particular areas of concern also allowed the Ombudsman to track the implementation of recommendations previously made as the legislation worked its way through the parliamentary machinery. For instance, in 2009, the Ombudsman for Children made observations on civil partnership and adoption legislation, highlighting the need for the legislation to reflect children's rights and the reality of children's lives. The Ombudsman had highlighted how legislative proposals for civil partnership ignored the children living in these relationships and made recommendations for their best interests to be taken into account (OCO, 2009, p. 47). When a later edition of the legislation came before the Ombudsman for comment, it was evident that the provisions had been amended in light of the recommendations previously made (OCO, 2014). Similarly, with respect to the reform of school admissions, the Ombudsman noted with regard to the redrafted legislation, that concerns previously raised by the institution had been addressed (OCO, 2015, 2019).

The Ombudsman for Children has also routinely commented or made invited submissions on matters of national policy in line with its mandate.

For instance, in 2012, the institution was invited to comment on the Draft National Consent Policy whose aim it was to provide one overarching policy for consent in health and social care services. Importantly, the Ombudsman used the opportunity to draw attention not only to the right of the child to be heard, but also to the substantive rights set out in Article 24 of the CRC regarding access to healthcare as well as the standards set out in the European Guidelines on Child-friendly Healthcare (OCO, 2012). Its submission on Better Outcomes, Brighter Futures: the National Policy Framework for Children and Young People also emphasised the need for the Framework to be fully underpinned by the state's obligations under the CRC, as did a similar submission on the National Action Plan on Trafficking in Human Beings made to the Department of Justice, Equality and Law Reform in 2008 (OCO, 2008).

The Ombudsman for Children has responded to general, public consultations to ensure children's rights are taken into account. For instance, in 2008, the Oireachtas Joint Committee on Health and Children issued an invitation for submissions on the issue of primary medical care in the community and the Ombudsman for Children made a submission based on issues that had come to the attention of the institution through its complaints and investigations work and its research and engagement with international monitoring mechanisms, including child protection, mental health services, children in care and access to therapeutic services (OCO, 2008). A similar approach was followed with regard to the Forum on Patronage and Pluralism in the Primary Sector which was the basis of an Ombudsman's submission to the Oireachtas Committee on Education (OCO, 2011) and in 2014, the Refugee Appeals Tribunal sought advice from the Ombudsman on its Draft Guidelines in relation to Child Applicants for Refugee Status (OCO, 2014).

The combined effect of the Ombudsman for Children's powers has enabled a thematic approach to the work of harmonising law and policy with the Convention from time to time. One concern that became the subject of sustained attention was the need to introduce a procedure for child death review. This matter was first brought to the attention of Government by the Ombudsman for Children in 2007, where following a scoping review, a submission was prepared that highlighted the need to establish a child death review mechanism like that found in other jurisdictions. Having received a positive response, the Ombudsman then progressed to examine international practice and consult with key stakeholders on the matter. This all culminated in a high-level seminar, in 2008, addressed by international experts, including the Commissioner for Children in New South Wales, and attended by various representatives of statutory bodies and agencies, designed to explore the model that would work best in Ireland. On foot of the recommendation made by the group, the Ombudsman produced an options paper setting out what aspects of child death are already being examined in Ireland at present and what issues should be considered in the context of establishing a single child death review mechanism. This paper was circulated to all key stakeholders, including the relevant Minister and in June 2009, the Ombudsman for Children presented the paper to a parliamentary committee with which it discussed its contents and recommendations. That year, the Government committed to establishing a mechanism for examining the deaths of children in care and in detention and although more limited in scope than that proposed, the development vindicated the initiative of the Ombudsman in taking on the issue. It is also a good illustration of how the institution can use its credibility to build consensus for reform on a difficult issue, across a wide stakeholder group (OCO, 2009).

The reach of the institution is evident from the variety of areas on which the Ombudsman has been consulted or has made submissions. For example, in 2013, the Ombudsman presented advice on the Courts Bill, which did not ostensibly impact children's rights but which, in addressing the transparency of court proceedings, clearly impacted on how family law and childcare matters are reported. The Ombudsman's submission helped to improve compliance of the legislation with human rights standards in this regard (OCO, 2013). Similarly, in the Ombudsman's submission on a new criminal law statute to address human trafficking and sexual offences, it was noted that the legislation was intended to promote compliance with a number of key instruments including the Optional Protocol to the CRC on the Sale of Children, Child Prostitution and Pornography, the UN Palermo Protocol on Trafficking and the Council of Europe Convention on Action Against Trafficking in Human Beings. While the submission welcomed that the legislation largely satisfied Ireland's international obligations, it did not adequately take into account the particular vulnerability of child victims or provide for their needs (OCO, 2007a). Time and again, as this illustrates therefore, the Ombudsman's advice has helped to shine an important light on legislative proposals from a children's rights perspective, even if its recommendations are not implemented. The institution also plays an important role in ensuring that children's views are directly taken into account in law and policymaking, avoiding the presumption that seeking the guidance of the Ombudsman is a substitute for consulting directly with children and young people. For instance, in its submission to Government on the age of digital consent, the Ombudsman recommended that 'meaningful consultation with children and young people' on the issue should take place (OCO, 2016, p. 61).

In summary, then, it is clear that the Ombudsman for Children has used the powers of the institution to guide, advise and inform both Government and Parliament about the children's rights implications of both draft and operating legislation, contributing to the 'thinking and clarification of various pieces of legislation' (OCO, 2015, pp. 6–7). The variety of issues that have been covered in the institution's submissions—from trafficking to court reporting, from child protection to gender recognition, from healthcare to adoption—illustrates both the range of areas where the law impacts on children's rights and the importance of ensuring that there is a dedicated office with the authority and the independence to make credible and informed observations on how to ensure the law is drafted and operates in harmony with international human rights obligations. In addition, the way in which the Ombudsman has carried out this function serves to link the different functions of the office in a strategic manner whereby, for instance, matters that are brought to its attention through the complaints function are used to illustrate the impact of the law on children's rights in submissions to Parliament. The Ombudsman's contributions in the area of child protection provide an excellent illustration of this point. For instance, when in 2006 the Ombudsman for Children made a written and oral submission to Parliament on child protection, addressing the need for reforms in the treatment of child witnesses in the criminal justice system, she noted that a confluence of important issues—a Supreme Court judgement, the enactment of legislation and the associated public debate on the issues—all indicated the need for a constitutional referendum to include explicit rights for children in the Constitution (OCO, 2006).

NHRI engagement with law and policymakers has a number of advantages. First, in drawing the attention of the legislature to the children's rights implications of proposed new laws, it has helped to promote greater harmonisation between national law and the CRC. This has been achieved by the Ombudsman for Children making submissions on legislative proposals that shed light on their weaknesses or gaps from a children's rights perspective as well as making recommendations, in line with the CRC, as to how these might be addressed. In this way, the contribution of the institution to the law-making process reminds Parliament that its power is not unfettered. Notwithstanding that the CRC is not part of national law, the Ombudsman for Children is there as a watchdog to ensure that its standards are met.

Second, in providing advice to Government on its proposed and draft legislation, the Ombudsman has established itself as a trusted and authoritative source on children's rights issues. This has helped to raise the profile of the institution and as a trusted body, the issues on which it advocates. Finally, and particularly pertinent to the own volition use of this power, the submissions of the Ombudsman for Children have helped to create a wider awareness of the implications for children's rights of legislative proposals, beyond those that might be perceived to impact directly on children. The advice provided has frequently been referenced and debated in the course of the Oireachtas' consideration of Bills affecting the rights and welfare of children. The advice provided by the Ombudsman for Children has contributed to and influenced parliamentary debate on draft legislation that affects the rights and welfare of children (OCO, 2010). The body's work has also reflected that, at times, 'the Oireachtas does not have the opportunity to consider broader issues that have a direct bearing on children which are related to the substance of a Bill but not explicitly addressed in it' (OCO, 2010, p. 9). For instance, in 2008, the Ombudsman's advice on the Immigration, Residence and Protection Bill 2008 was presented to the Oireachtas Joint Committee on Justice, Equality, Defence and Women's Rights (OCO, 2008). Here, the Ombudsman's advice was that while the Bill had some positive aspects, it did not sufficiently take account of the particular vulnerability of children and of the need to provide them with special assistance and protection. Specific issues raised in the advice included the needs of separated children seeking asylum, the age determination process, family reunification, detention of asylum seekers and child trafficking (OCO, 2008).

Although the role played by the Ombudsman for Children in advising and guiding law and policymaking in line with children's rights has undoubtedly been influential, it has not always been successful in altering the course of legislative proposals or ensuring adequate consideration is given to the rights of the child. Although a comprehensive analysis of the impact of the institution in this area is beyond the scope of this work—and should clearly be a priority of the institution itself—there are examples of where the guidance has not been taken into account. For instance, in its 2016 Annual Report the Ombudsman commented with respect to the Criminal Law Sexual Offences Bill 2015 that 'we remained concerned that many of our recommendations had not been incorporated into the Bill' (OCO, 2016, p. 63). This can occur across all areas where there are, naturally, competing considerations or where the matter is one of particular sensitivity or controversy. For example, reform of the law on adoption has been particularly protracted and difficult and despite recommendations of the Ombudsman for Children, such as those made with respect to the Adoption Bill in 2009, matters relating to identity and tracing, among others, have not yet been satisfactorily resolved (OCO, 2009, 2015). In certain areas, the sheer volume of the recommendations provided by the Ombudsman—while itself a message about the proposal's compliance with children's rights—may make it difficult for Government to take them all into account. For instance, in 2016, the institution made a submission to the national Child and Family Agency on the Review of the National Leaving and Aftercare Policy 2011, providing 66 recommendations across 26 areas (OCO, 2016).

As there is no duty on Parliament to report back to the Ombudsman on whether and to what extent the advice provided has been taken into account, there is no easy way to track the impact of the institution in this respect. Other jurisdictions have introduced child impact assessment mechanisms as means to improve adherence in the parliamentary process to the rights of children (Williams, 2012). The introduction of such a mechanism in Ireland would go some way to remedying this gap, ensuring a greater level of transparency and accountability in the law-making process from a children's rights perspective.

## 5.4 Constitutional Reform

While the Ombudsman for Children has been involved in a sustained and systematic manner in the reform of particular areas of law from a children's rights perspective—child protection and education are two obvious examples—its role in the reform of the Constitution is an excellent example of the kind of influence that an NHRI for children can have. In Ireland, the Constitution can only be amended by public referendum and for many years civil society, human rights and children's sector groups, legal practitioners and academics had expressed concern about the absence of children's rights from the Constitution (O'Mahony & Kilkelly, 2007). The newly appointed Ombudsman for Children had raised this matter with Government in 2005 and again in 2006 and in the midst of multiple reports documenting the abuse and ill-treatment of children, announced its intention to propose a constitutional amendment on children's rights to the people, launching a consultation to agree appropriate wording (OCO, 2006). The Ombudsman submitted the first advice on the matter in 2005, recommending an amendment to the Constitution to grant express rights to children, in the definition of which Government was recommended to consider the rights in the CRC. In particular, the Ombudsman recommended that the Constitution should be amended to ensure that the right of children to have their welfare protected is given the paramountcy it deserves (OCO, 2005b). The Ombudsman next advised Government on the proposed legislation to amend the Constitution, also submitting, on their own volition, a special report to the Oireachtas on the matter, the first time the Children's Ombudsman submitted such a report (OCO, 2007a, 2007b). This recommended the inclusion in the Constitution of an express statement of the rights of the child, the inclusion in the Constitution of the best interests principle, the inclusion of a duty to support families and a duty to act in a proportionate manner in this regard. Engagement with the relevant parliamentary committee, during 2008, highlighted the importance of focusing not just on the courts, but on areas of administrative decision-making which, the Ombudsman pointed out, presented a more 'insidious obstacle' as a place where decisions are made that can have 'a profound effect on the lives of children and their families' (OCO, 2008, p. 9). For this reason, the Ombudsman observed that

> the most common obstacles to the development of a culture that respects children's rights are the absence of any positive obligation on administrative authorities to consider a child's best interests and a consistent absence of the views of the child in decisions that affect them. (OCO, 2008, p. 9)

These concerns were reiterated in 2011 when the Ombudsman recalled, drawing on the work of the institution's complaint function, the large numbers of children impacted by decision-making by civil and public administration (OCO, 2011). Ultimately, however, the Ombudsman's advocacy on this particular issue was unsuccessful.

In 2008, a debate had emerged around whether to split what was becoming an increasingly complex proposal into distinct elements, holding a referendum on each one beginning with the issue that had been the subject of a Supreme Court judgment namely the re-introduction of an offence of absolute or strict liability for sexual offences in connection with children. It was proposed to leave the remaining issues—including making express provision for the rights and best interests of children—to some later point. In addressing this proposal, the Ombudsman publicly highlighted the risks of treating child protection separately from broader children's rights issues, remarking on the Ombudsman's duty to call out publicly the concern she had expressed in private, that of 'growing political pressure' to pursue the amendment with regard to matters of child protection only (OCO, 2008, p. 10). The Ombudsman's view that—that the Referendum must deal more comprehensively with children's rights and not the more limited issue of child protection—received a cool political response. However, it was to be an important intervention in what was undoubtedly a complex and in some respects unsatisfactory process of reform (O'Mahony, 2016).

Although the report of the relevant parliamentary committee in 2009 appeared to put the broader children's rights referendum back on track, with wide parliamentary support, the publication of its draft wording in 2010 led again to expressions of opposition, this time from civil servants in the ministries for health, justice and education who considered that placing the best interests of the child in the Constitution would have 'unintended consequences' (OCO, 2010, p. 10). This claim was flatly rejected by the Ombudsman in their contributions, who continued to press for a constitutional amendment that included the general principles of the CRC, while advocating for the meaningful change in children's lives that such constitutional expression could bring (OCO, 2010). A further important intervention was made by the office in 2011, with respect to the anxiety, circulating publicly, that parents' rights would be diluted by inserting children's rights into the Constitution. According to the Ombudsman, contrary to the view that recognition of children's rights conflicts with the rights of parents,

> If there is one thing that has been confirmed by our eight years of work, it is that parents are by far the strongest and most tenacious advocates for children. This is why the children that I continue to be most concerned about are children without parental care, the children who do not have that tenacious parent fighting their corner. (OCO, 2011, p. 8)

The Ombudsman also remarked that the constitutional amendment, even if successful, would not be a panacea and that challenges would continue to be faced by children in the 'practical realisation of their rights on a daily basis by service providers' (OCO, 2011, p. 8). Nonetheless, the Ombudsman argued, holding a referendum on children's rights provided Ireland with a chance to be 'a leader on children's rights globally' (OCO, 2011, p. 8).

The campaign was refreshed in 2012 when, partnered with a former Supreme Court judge, the Ombudsman continued to present their views at the highest level of Government (OCO, 2012), highlighting the need for substantive CRC rights to be included in the Constitution. When the wording for the proposed Article 42A was finally published, accepted to be a diluted form from that recommended by the Oireachtas Committee in 2010 (Joint Committee on the Constitutional Amendment on Children, 2010), it included important elements from a children's rights perspective. In particular, it included recognition of the rights of the child with a corresponding duty on the state to vindicate those rights, a duty to make legislative provision for the best interests of the child to be paramount and the right of the child to be heard in child protection, adoption and private family law proceedings, as well as amendments to existing adoption and alternative care provisions designed to enable children's rights to be taken into account.

The amendment was passed by referendum on 10 November 2012, although an unsuccessful constitutional challenge meant that it was 2016 before it took effect. The Ombudsman for Children was not permitted to participate in the public campaign for the referendum due to a legal prohibition on the use of public funds for this purpose but it is clear nonetheless that the institution had played a very significant role—especially at key points in the journey—in the reform that was ultimately achieved. Others have considered the success of the Irish effort to constitutionalise children's rights (O'Mahony, 2020), which had many contributing factors and actors, from civil society, academia and public life. However, two points fall to be made about the importance of the Ombudsman's role. First, it is evident that the impact of the Ombudsman for Children was keenly felt throughout the decade long process that led up to the referendum. It was a key priority early on for the institution and this early influence with stakeholders helped to reinforce the credibility of the institution during the process and the relevance and importance of the constitutional issue more generally. Second, although the wording is weaker than some wanted, there were key points in the long campaign where it could have been diluted further or even derailed altogether.

The influence and credibility of the Ombudsman for Children meant that this did not happen as the independence, authority and integrity of the institution gave it an unrivalled platform from which to advocate for the strongest possible protection of children's rights. At the same time, while considerable satisfaction can be derived from the inclusion of the express recognition of children's rights in Article 42A(1) and the references to Articles 3 and 12 of the CRC, the absence from the amendment of administrative decision-making has limited the relevance of the amendment to larger numbers of children in areas of public decision-making that impacts on their lives.

## 5.5 Conclusion

The Ombudsman for Children has been clearly positioned as a stakeholder in the parliamentary process, with specific duties to provide advice and guidance on proposed, draft and operating legislation from a children's rights perspective. The breadth of children's rights concerns means that this is a potentially endless responsibility, and clearly choices have had to be made as to the areas where the institution can have most effect. Not surprisingly, perhaps, matters of child protection, reform of family law and education have been most prominent in this regard, with important contributions made too in the areas of gender recognition and criminal law. There is no doubt that the wide range of legislative issues on which the Ombudsman has made interventions has raised the profile of children's rights in Irish law and policy, where the credibility of the institution—derived largely from its complaints function and its regular interaction with children themselves—has enabled it to bring influence to bear on particularly sensitive and difficult subjects. This was especially evident during the campaign to amend the Constitution where at key moments the strong children's rights position adopted by the Ombudsman—although it risked isolation from the children's sector—helped to keep the broad direction of the amendment on track.

While engagement in this area from the Ombudsman for Children has undoubtedly increased awareness about children's rights among legislators, it is difficult to say with greater precision what impact its submissions have had. In this regard, the institution should look to document, systematically and with more detail, the changes brought about on foot of its advice (and not), perhaps putting in place a tracking mechanism so that this process can be better understood. More generally, it is perhaps timely to campaign for the introduction of a children's rights impact assessment mechanism. Learning from our nearest neighbours in Wales could be instructive in this regard (Williams, 2012). Such a measure would help to formalise parliamentary responsiveness to children's rights issues during the legislative process and require greater initiative by Parliament with respect to engagement with CRC provisions and principles. This would be an important complement to the mandate of the Ombudsman for Children in ensuring greater harmonisation of national law and policy with the Convention.

## References


Joint Committee on the Constitutional Amendment on Children. (2010). *Twenty-Eight Amendment of the Constitution Bill 2007: Proposal for a Constitutional Amendment to Strengthen Children's Rights, Final Report*. The Stationery Office.

Kilkelly, U. (2007). *Barriers to the realisation of children's rights in Ireland*. Ombudsman for Children's Office.

O'Mahony, C. (2016). Falling short of expectations: The 2012 children amendment, from drafting to referendum. *Irish Political Studies, 31*(2), 252–281.

O'Mahony, C. (2020). The promises and pitfalls of constitutionalizing children's rights. In J. G. Dwyer (Ed.), *The Oxford handbook of children and the law* (pp. 872–898). Oxford University Press.

O'Mahony, C., & Kilkelly, U. (2007). The proposed children's rights amendment: Running to stand still? *Irish Journal of Family Law, 2*, 19–25.

Ombudsman for Children. (2005a). *Annual report 2005*. Ombudsman for Children's Office.

Ombudsman for Children. (2005b, January). *Submission to the All-Party Oireachtas Committee on the Constitution*. Ombudsman for Children's Office.

Ombudsman for Children. (2006). *Respecting children: Annual report of the Ombudsman for Children's Office April 2005–December 2006*. Ombudsman for Children's Office.

Ombudsman for Children. (2007a). *Hearing children: Annual report of the Ombudsman for Children's Office January 2007-December 2007*. Ombudsman for Children's Office.

Ombudsman for Children. (2007b). *Report to the Oireachtas on the Twenty-Eighth Amendment of the Constitution Bill 2007*, March 2007. Ombudsman for Children's Office.

Ombudsman for Children. (2008). *Annual report 2008*. Ombudsman for Children's Office.

Ombudsman for Children. (2009). *Annual report 2009.* Ombudsman for Children's Office.
Ombudsman for Children. (2010). *Annual report 2010.* Ombudsman for Children's Office.
Ombudsman for Children. (2011). *Annual report 2011.* Ombudsman for Children's Office.
Ombudsman for Children. (2012). *Annual report 2012.* Ombudsman for Children's Office.
Ombudsman for Children. (2013). *Annual report 2013.* Ombudsman for Children's Office.
Ombudsman for Children. (2014). *Annual report 2014.* Ombudsman for Children's Office.
Ombudsman for Children. (2015). *Annual report 2015.* Ombudsman for Children's Office.
Ombudsman for Children. (2016). *Annual report 2016.* Ombudsman for Children's Office.
Ombudsman for Children. (2018). *Annual report 2018.* Ombudsman for Children's Office.
Ombudsman for Children. (2019). *Progress for children: Annual report 2019.* Ombudsman for Children's Office.
Ombudsman for Children. (2021). *Submission to the 39th session of the Universal Periodic Review Working Group.* Dublin: Ombudsman for Children's Office.
Ombudsman for Children Act 2002.
UN Convention on the Rights of the Child (CRC) 1989.
UN Committee on the Rights of the Child. (2002). *General Comment No. 2 (2002): The role of independent national human rights institutions in the promotion and protection of the rights of the child*, 15 November 2002, CRC/GC/2002/2.
UN General Assembly. (1993). Principles relating to the status of national institutions (Paris Principles). UN Doc. A/RES/48/134.
Williams, J. (2012). General legislative measures of implementation: Individual claims, 'public officer's law' and a case study on the UNCRC in Wales. *The International Journal of Children's Rights, 20*(2), 224–240.

CHAPTER 6

# Complaints and Investigations

**Abstract** In line with international standards, the power to investigate complaints is considered one of the 'major' powers of the Ombudsman for Children, and it is one of the cornerstones of its legislative mandate. As a key function in the protection of children's rights, the Ombudsman considers approximately 1500 complaints annually from children or their representatives regarding their treatment by public bodies on issues concerning education, healthcare, child protection and housing. While many individual complaints have been resolved to the satisfaction of the parties, the nature and range of complaints made and the responses of public bodies can raise systemic concerns that warrant proactive approaches by the Ombudsman for Children, connected with the institution's duty to promote, as well as to protect, the rights of children. Thematic reviews and special reports, among other initiatives, have helped to address the fact that the Ombudsman's recommendations are not legally binding although it is clear that the absence of a legal power—such as to intervene as an amicus friend in litigation—would strengthen the role of the institution in this regard.

**Keywords** Complaints handling · Investigations · Public body · Children's rights · Education · Health



U. Kilkelly and E. Logan, *National Independent Human Rights Institutions for Children*,
https://doi.org/10.1007/978-3-030-80275-2_6

## 6.1 Introduction

The decision to establish Ireland's national human rights institution (NHRI) for children as an 'ombudsman', with capacity to consider complaints from children about their treatment by public bodies, was critical to creating a 'more effective champion' for children's rights (Williams, 2005, p. 50). In line with the expectations of the international community, as set out in the Paris Principles (UN General Assembly, 1993) and General Comment No. 2 of the Committee on the Rights of the Child (2002, para. 13), the Ombudsman for Children has the power to receive complaints and conduct investigations, including of its own volition, into the treatment of a child. A study of the operation of the institution would be incomplete therefore without an analysis of how this power has been used to effect change in children's rights. That is perhaps one of the anomalies here, i.e. that the mandate of the Ombudsman for Children is to promote and protect the rights of the child whereas the complaint function is limited to actions that are considered, in general terms, to be contrary to fair and sound administration. While these purposes are not necessarily mutually exclusive, it is categorically not the purpose of the Ombudsman for Children under its founding legislation to investigate breaches of children's rights, the implications of which distinction have perhaps not been adequately explored to date.

This chapter sets out the powers of the Ombudsman for Children to receive and investigate complaints against public bodies on behalf of children. Against a backdrop of increased recourse to this function by and on behalf of children, it considers the areas in which complaints are received, highlighting some of the outcomes achieved on behalf of the children involved. Aware that the resolution of individual complaints, while important, is of limited value in effecting broader systemic change in the treatment of children, the chapter will also detail the connections between the different aspects of the Ombudsman's role, drawing connections with complaints and the broader duty to promote children's rights. The chapter will also outline an initiative undertaken by the office in the area of complaints handling, which has sought to raise awareness among public bodies more generally as to how to ensure complaints are handled in line with children's rights standards.

## 6.2 The Powers of the Ombudsman for Children

The authority of the Ombudsman for Children to investigate complaints made by or on behalf of children has been described as a 'major power' (Martin, 2004, p. 63). As set out in the Ombudsman for Children Act 2002 (s. 8), the institution can investigate complaints about any 'action' taken by or on behalf of a public body which appears to the Ombudsman following preliminary investigation, to satisfy one or more criteria. In particular, the Act requires that the action has or may have 'adversely affected a child' and separately, was or may have been, 'taken without proper authority', 'taken on irrelevant grounds', 'the result of negligence or carelessness', 'based on erroneous or incomplete information', 'improperly discriminatory', 'based on an undesirable administrative practice' or 'otherwise contrary to fair or sound administration' (s. 8). Based on the founding legislation for the general public services Ombudsman, which has interpreted these terms interchangeably and loosely in an association with 'fairness', it was anticipated that the Ombudsman for Children would take a similar approach (Martin, 2004, p. 65). Importantly, the Act does not prescribe the procedure to be followed in the investigation of a complaint, leaving it to the discretion of the institution to put such appropriate procedures in place. The Act (s. 6) does require, however, that in the performance of the complaint and investigation function, the Ombudsman must 'have regard to the best interests of the child concerned and shall, in so far as practicable, give due consideration, having regard to the age and understanding of the child, to his or her wishes'. While the fairness and integrity of the overall process requires a certain rigour to be applied to the investigations process, Martin highlights the importance of 'informality' which 'can result in substantial success particularly where children are concerned' (Martin, 2004, p. 69).

Significantly, the Ombudsman for Children does not have to wait for a complaint to be received from a child to initiate an investigation, which can be done of its own volition where this is 'warranted' (Ombudsman for Children Act, 2002, s. 10). The Ombudsman may decide not to investigate or may discontinue the investigation if the complaint appears to be 'trivial or vexatious', if the complainant has insufficient interest or fails to pursue or accept a remedy with respect to the matter or if the passage of time makes redress 'impossible or impracticable' (Ombudsman for Children Act, 2002, s. 10). The exclusions under this part of the Act have been addressed in Chapter 3 above, most of which have now been resolved. Nevertheless, it remains the case that the making of a complaint is subject to a two-year time limit and is precluded inter alia where the matter is the subject of civil proceedings (Ombudsman for Children Act, 2002, s. 10).

In terms of the proposed remedies, where an action has been found to be contrary to sound and fair administration, the Ombudsman can recommend to the public body concerned that the matter be given further consideration, that measures are taken to remedy, mitigate or alter the adverse effect of the action or that the reasons for taking the action be given. No adverse finding will be made without the person impacted being given a right of reply, in order to ensure that fair procedures are followed, but in any event the recommendation of the Ombudsman shall be communicated to the parties. Martin (2004, pp. 66–67) notes that the approach set out in the Act is reflective of the fact that the Ombudsman's powers are not to be viewed as 'adversarial or confrontational', but instead and unlike the courts are considered more in the vein of an 'inquisitorial, flexible and private process of inquiry'. At the same time, the Ombudsman for Children cannot make binding findings or recommendations and, in this respect, falls short of the expectations of international standards (Rees, 2010). Nonetheless, the Ombudsman has sweeping powers in the performance of this function and can (Ombudsman for Children Act, 2002, s. 14) compel a person to produce any 'document or thing' in their possession relevant to the investigation. This undoubtedly makes the institution a powerful force when investigating actions of public bodies on behalf of children. Consistent with this authority, the Ombudsman can under s. 13(5) of the Act choose to issue a 'special report' if, for instance, 'the same complaints arise consistently, suggesting systemic faults' (Rees, 2010, p. 423). This acts as an important and explicit connection between the complaints function of the Ombudsman for Children and the institution's wider advocacy and promotion functions.

## 6.3 The Ombudsman for Children's Approach to Complaints

With the establishment of the institution the Ombudsman began accepting complaints almost immediately and in its first Annual Report explained some of the elements of how it intended to approach this function, noting that it was the policy of the office to respect existing local complaints mechanisms and procedures in order to afford the body concerned the opportunity to respond. In noting the extent of its powers under the legislation, including to compel the production of documents, the Ombudsman noted that '[t]here is no doubt that these powers must be exercised with great care and responsibility' and went on to advise that when considering complaints, the office would consider the best interests of the child in the matter and 'at all times' have regard for 'the dignity and human rights of everyone we deal with and ensure that the Office is accessible to all' (Ombudsman for Children [OCO], 2005, p. 11).

These principles were built upon in the publication by the Ombudsman in 2007 of a Guide to the office's complaints procedures (OCO, 2007a). This provided information for complainants about the Ombudsman's 'independent and impartial complaint handling procedure' and advised that in handling complaints, the Ombudsman is 'neither an advocate for any child nor an adversary of any body complained against' (OCO, 2007a, p. 7). In this regard, it noted that in the context of examining a complaint, the Ombudsman aims to support the parties to 'arrive at a mutual understanding of the complaint and to resolve the complaint informally' (OCO, 2007a, p. 8). It went onto say that when investigating a complaint, the Ombudsman seeks to resolve it based on 'its informed understanding of the complaint' and that when concluding an investigation, it will issue 'an investigation statement' and 'a set of recommendations as appropriate'. It committed only to publish such a statement if it considers there is 'learning which may impact on bodies other than the one investigated' in which case both parties would be fully informed of this decision in advance (OCO, 2007a, p. 8). According to the Guide, the Ombudsman based its complaints handling on ten principles—best interests of the child, independence, impartiality, integrity, consistency and flexibility, proportionality, transparency, accessibility and inclusion, participation, and a professional and results-focused approach (OCO, 2007a). The Guide also set out how the office expected to take account of its responsibilities under the legislation (s. 6) to have regard to the best interests of the child and the right of the child to be heard in its investigation of any complaints. In particular, it set out factors that would guide its consideration of the child's participation in the process, such as whether this was a procedural necessity, whether the Ombudsman can provide the necessary support to enable such participation, and whether the child in fact wants to be involved in the process. The Guide also set out the parameters to guide the consideration to be given to the views of the child, such as whether the child's wishes were consistent with their best interests, whether these wishes had been expressed freely, and whether the child's wishes impose obligations or interfere with the rights of others (OCO, 2007a).

In 2009, the Ombudsman supplemented this guidance to public bodies with resources for children and young people designed to provide them with information on how to complain to the Ombudsman, while also providing information about what happens when a complaint is received (OCO, 2009a). The multi-media resources, developed in consultation with a children's organisation, comprised three short films telling the story of three complaints to the office and the effect of their outcomes on the children involved. These resources were distributed nationally to children and youth organisations around the country with a view to raising awareness among young people of the complaint function of the office.

In the intervening years, as the number of complaints has grown, the Ombudsman's approach to complaints has evolved to become more strategic, with the focus moving to more systemic issues or illustrative cases. Data about the number of complaints investigated, compared to the number received, are published in the Annual Report, however a more rigorous analysis of complaints versus investigations would help to better understand the strategic role of the institution, especially given the concern that the complaint function would risk the office being swamped with individual cases (see Chapter 2).

From time to time, the Ombudsman for Children has expressed frustration at slow or difficult engagement with some public bodies implicated in a complaint, a matter that can delay the investigation. Measures have been taken to try to resolve these difficulties by strengthening the liaison arrangements in order to ensure more timely communication and flow of information (OCO, 2008). In some circumstances, including one where the public body in question took legal action to prevent the Ombudsman investigating the matter, the delay was both prolonged and according to the Ombudsman, deeply distressing for the complainant (OCO, 2009b). The Ombudsman has frequently noted the resistance among some public bodies to the investigation function, with correspondence focusing on the investigative remit of the office and in some instances coming from the body's legal representatives in the first instance (OCO, 2010). While the Ombudsman has noted the risks that this poses to the open and transparent oversight over public bodies which the institution provides, it is perhaps useful to consider why an Ombudsman's investigation might prompt such a response.

While there are no doubt cynical reasons why an investigation might be resisted by some public bodies, others may indeed have genuine questions about the nature of the investigation, its scope and the likely knock-on impact of the process on the operation of the body, the legal rights of individuals affected and matters associated with the broader public interest. A review of annual reports indicates that the school setting appears to raise a particular concern both from the perspective of the number of complaints being received and the investigation of complaints by the Ombudsman. While it was originally intended that schools would only be subject to an investigation by the Ombudsman where local grievance procedures have been exhausted by the complainant (Glendenning, 2004), for various reasons this is not always the case. In some instances, the matters are relatively minor in nature, such as the school authorities failing to properly articulate the reasons for their decision beyond recording 'complaint has not been substantiated', perhaps making decisions that are in fact based on sound and reasonable grounds hard to accept by the complainant (OCO, 2010, pp. 41–42). In other cases, the matters are more serious and might concern, for instance, poor adherence to the national child protection framework, failure to have adequate procedures in place to deal with school bullying and so on. While these issues have been addressed by the Ombudsman through engagement with national education bodies including the Department of Education, the importance of ensuring that schools have robust and effective complaint mechanisms cannot be overstated. More recently, in this regard, the Ombudsman welcomed proposals to legislate for more streamlined complaints mechanisms in schools acknowledging the potential of the Education (Student and Parent Charter) Bill 2016 to 'increase consistency around complaints handling in all schools' and to provide the Ombudsman for Children with 'additional powers to deal with complaints that relate to schools' (OCO, 2016, p. 25). Although the capacity of the Bill to improve transparency and inclusiveness in schools was highlighted by the Ombudsman when the revised Bill was published in 2019, concern was expressed that the requirement in the Bill that school complaint procedures would have to be exhausted before a complaint could be made to the Ombudsman, would cause significant difficulties for children trying to have their concerns addressed (OCO, 2019).

Martin argued at the time that the Children's Ombudsman was established that the post holder would have to 'adopt the approach undertaken by the public service Ombudsman of sometimes looking beyond individual complaints and investigating, in a non-adversarial way, possible systemic weaknesses within public bodies, hospitals and schools' (2004, p. 80). The Ombudsman has taken a number of approaches in this regard. First, it has issued a number of Special Reports, arising out of individual complaints in the areas of child protection (OCO, 2006) and housing (OCO, 2012a), for instance, drawing attention to systemic and structural problems in the implementation of national law and policy and making significant and detailed recommendations for improvements related to the consistency, transparency and co-ordination of services across the area. Second, in dealings with the public bodies it has sought to bring systemic issues of concern to their attention in order to address the stem of individual complaints continuing to arise. For instance, following a complaint from a child in foster care with profound special needs, the Ombudsman engaged throughout 2011 with the relevant authority as to how to translate the complaint into meaningful change for children and families (OCO, 2011a). Clearly, by bringing together a number or series of individual complaints so as to highlight the need for more structural reforms is an important way to fulfil the Ombudsman's duty to promote as well as to protect the rights of the child. Third, the Ombudsman has engaged in thematic reviews of complaints in order to identify broader issues arising from the individual complaints process, publishing learning annually in its reports to parliament. Combined with its analysis of 'emerging issues' or 'significant issues' as set out in the Annual Reports, this has enabled more considered and system-wide reflections on both issues of concern from a children's rights perspective and the responses from public bodies to the resolution of complaints, critically examining the trends in this regard. For instance, in 2010, the Ombudsman reported the trend of the Department of Education to respond to its recommendations arising out of complaints by undertaking to take them into account in its internal policy review processes. As the Ombudsman noted, this can have multiple effects, including making it less likely that action arising from the child's complaint will be effective and timely in addressing the rights and needs of the children concerned (OCO, 2010). These have been used effectively from year to year to raise the profile of issues of either persistent or grave concern, leading also to Special Reports and other own volition investigations in areas like the treatment of children in alternative care (OCO, 2013a, 2018a), child protection (Charles, 2009; OCO, 2013b), housing and homelessness (e.g. OCO, 2012a, 2012b), and disability (OCO, 2011b, 2012c). Annual Reports and other ad hoc publications also feature case studies designed to illustrate both the challenges that children face accessing services and supports in line with their needs, and showcasing how effective the Ombudsman complaint function can be in achieving redress and resolution in respect of children's complaints (OCO, 2019). In the absence of legally binding recommendations, these mechanisms are an essential way to maximise the potential of the individual complaint process to bring about systemic change.

The third approach used in this regard is a focus by the Ombudsman on how to support better decision-making and complaints handling by public bodies. In addition to drawing attention to positive experiences through the publishing of case studies, the Ombudsman published an updated guide to child-centred complaints handling in 2018. Informed by the experience of handling complaints and by international research on complaints mechanisms and children's rights standards like those set out in the European Guidelines on Child-friendly Justice (Council of Europe, 2010), the Guidance sets out good practice in responding to complaints made by, or on behalf of, children (OCO, 2018b). The Guide (OCO, 2018b) details seven core principles as follows:

1. *Openness and accessibility*
   This involves adopting an open and flexible approach to meeting the needs of children which requires a number of measures to be taken, such as offering a free complaint handling service, informal and formal complaint options, and flexibility in accommodating specific needs as well as communication methods. It also involves encouraging feedback and learning from complaints to improve the service and recommends that children should be involved in developing accessible information materials about the process.
2. *Best interests of the child*
   The best interests of the child must be a primary consideration at all stages of the complaints process and no harm or distress must be caused to the child. A multi-disciplinary approach should be taken in deciding what may be in the child's best interests, and a problem-solving approach is encouraged to determine the best outcome. How the best interests of the child were examined and upheld should be documented at all stages of the process.

3. *Participation of children*
   The participation of children in the complaints process should be prioritised—seeking and giving due weight to their views, taking into account their age and maturity. Children's participation must be voluntary and where they want such involvement, they should be supported to express their views including via a support person if that is their preference. It is important to consider the barriers obstructing children's participation, including power imbalances, fear of reprisal in making a complaint, and lack of trust in authority or the complaints system.
4. *Transparency and communication*
   Children and their representatives must understand the options available and the complaint process itself by ensuring that there is in place a clear policy and procedure for: dealing with complaints; informing children and their representatives about the options available and the complaint process; providing guidance and support; acknowledging all complaints promptly and in writing; and providing regular, clear and accessible updates.
5. *Timeliness*
   Complaints made by or on behalf of children must be prioritised, with the complaint process completed efficiently and without unnecessary delay. Safety and welfare concerns require an urgent response.
6. *Fairness*
   Children must have access to a fair and impartial complaints process. Complaints must be investigated fully by reviewing all relevant information, considering the views of relevant parties, and assessing the impact on children's rights. Separate meetings should be held with the different parties involved to ensure an inclusive and equitable approach to their participation in the complaints process and children must also have access to an independent appeals procedure.
7. *Monitoring and review*
   This principle requires maintaining accurate, complete, and up-to-date records of all complaints; monitoring and reviewing complaints to inform best practice; and conducting regular reviews of complaints policy and procedures (including considering feedback from children).

## 6.4 Substance of Complaints Before the Ombudsman for Children

With the appointment of the Ombudsman for Children in 2004, the institution began to accept complaints almost immediately, considering 177 complaints in its first year of operations (OCO, 2005). The majority of these complaints concerned education (51.4%), including special educational needs, material conditions in schools and the handling of bullying concerns. 16.4% concerned health issues, mainly access to services and supports, and a further 26.6% concerned matters of child protection, social welfare entitlements and other concerns relating to custody and asylum and immigration matters (OCO, 2005). A thematic review of the complaints identified that complainants encountered a range of administrative problems, including a lack of information about how to complain, delay in decision-making or the handling of a request or complaint by a public body, and the complexity of accessing services, especially for those with additional needs.

From its modest beginnings in 2004, the complaint function has continued to grow and expand, doubling in numbers from 2005 (357) to 2007 (742), almost doubling again by 2011 when 1393 new complaints were received. By 2019, the numbers had proven to be relatively consistent, year on year, with an approximate number of 1500 complaints received annually (OCO, 2019). There is consistency also in the proportion of complaints submitted by parents—which continues to be approximately 80% of those submitted—with children submitting an average of about 3% (OCO, 2019). Finally, the complaints continue to cluster around a number of themes with 2019 figures showing a typical complaints profile, with education continuing to dominate, at close to half of all complaints received, health services attracting around 14% and family support and care about 20% (OCO, 2019). Although the picture has changed from 2011, when complaints about education comprised 41% of the total received and health made up 34%, the overall proportions have not changed significantly—the largest number of complaints remains about education, followed by health services. Smaller numbers of complaints are made relating to housing at just 5%, justice at 6%, and finance and welfare at 3%, with the 2019 figures again being mostly typical of the trend year on year (e.g. OCO, 2019).

The complaints received by the Ombudsman for Children cover a range of issues across the full gambit of education, health services, housing, child protection and care. They fall loosely into the following categories. First, they include complaints regarding decisions taken by public bodies like education, health or social services, refusing children's access to or determining children ineligible for particular services, supports, benefits or care programmes. In some cases, the decision (i.e. the refusal) is the subject of the complaint, while in others the matter of access is either unresolved or inconclusive. For instance, this might include a decision refusing a child access to school transport (OCO, 2008), for which they consider themselves eligible; or failure to provide certainty, within a timely manner, with regard to a child's access to housing or to living supports (OCO, 2008). In healthcare, this category includes delays accessing time and developmentally-sensitive services, such as speech and language therapy, psychology assessment and child and adolescent mental health services (OCO, 2009b, p. 28). It might address the failure to share information, ensure proper record keeping and it can include situations where children do not receive the services to which they are entitled either because they do not meet the criteria or because the services they need are unavailable due to a lack of resources, staffing or regional variations (OCO, 2007b). The second category of complaints relates to situations where the public body does not address or resolve a complaint in a satisfactory manner about the child's treatment. These types of complaints come to the Ombudsman for Children because the complainant's attempt to have them resolved locally by the public body has been unsuccessful. This may arise because the public body's complaints procedures are unclear or inaccessible (OCO, 2008), because there is delay in addressing or resolving the complaint or where the outcome is considered by the complainant to be unsatisfactory or unfair. For example, in one instance, a school's handling of an allegation of inappropriate treatment by a teacher of a child demonstrated that appropriate procedures to govern the investigation of the incident by the school were not in place (OCO, 2009b).

The situations that give rise to complaints to the Ombudsman are thus incredibly varied and diverse and undoubtedly impact most severely on those who require specialist services and supports, or who are particularly vulnerable or face disadvantage. For instance, many of the children complaining to the Ombudsman for Children directly are in the care of the state with concerns about what would normally be considered basic entitlements related to their care, such as the failure to include children in their placement planning, to appoint them a social worker or to ensure they have access to aftercare supports or housing on leaving care (OCO, 2009b). In such instances, the local complaint procedures should in most cases be remedying the concerns without necessitating recourse to the Ombudsman for Children.

## 6.5 Improving Administrative Practice Among Public Bodies

Thematic analyses of the complaints undertaken by the Ombudsman for Children illustrate the challenges that many children and their families face in seeking access to supports and services that meet the child's needs. In many instances, slow, inflexible and bureaucratic administration is a source of much frustration and anxiety for them, and the Ombudsman has also observed as a particular concern the impact of the fragmentation of services, whereby individual services or supports fall within the remit of different offices (e.g. education or health), but the child requires an integrated service on the basis of need (OCO, 2009b). According to the Ombudsman for Children, the absence of a child-focused approach was exacerbated by a tightening of resources that made flexibility less likely, combined with a lack of communication or inter-agency working across public services that was contrary to the child's best interests under the CRC (OCO, 2009b, pp. 29–30).

Each complaint that is resolved by the Ombudsman to the satisfaction of the parties will normally involve putting in place an individualised and agreed set of measures, in line with the recommendations from the investigation. Ideally, these complaints will be resolved by extending to the child in question—and sometimes others who are eligible—by agreement with the public body, access to the service, support or benefit that the child needs. This might include access to school transport, to appropriate educational supports or to a health diagnosis or specialist service. This resolution of the complaint in some such manner will meet the expectations of the complainant in most cases. For the Ombudsman to fulfil the institution's wider statutory duty to protect and promote the rights of the child, however, additional measures may be required in order to prevent similar situations arising in the future. This might involve for instance the adoption of new or revised policy, clarification of a procedure, improved transparency in eligibility criteria or the allocation of resources to widen the accessibility of services or supports. Local complaint mechanisms might be put in place and more widely communicated, and protocols developed to ensure all appropriate steps in such procedures are followed. Training might be undertaken to sensitise decision-makers to the needs of the child and clear procedural guidance developed to guide staff discharging their administrative functions with a view to ensuring that decision-making is equitable, fair and timely. Inter-agency protocols might be agreed to improve communication and collaboration across services (OCO, 2010).

The routine analysis of complaints by the Ombudsman has identified the gaps and shortcomings in administrative decision-making and processes that impact on children's fair treatment and access to state services and supports. However, in order to understand the children's rights implications of their experiences, the Ombudsman for Children commissioned research to undertake an analysis of ten individual complaints from a children's rights perspective (Kilkelly, 2011). The study drew, in particular, on international children's rights standards, specifically the CRC, in the study of the complaints and used this framework to identify a number of common themes. The analysis highlighted the limited oversight of administrative decision-making in place and the lack of mechanisms for challenging the decisions made. Where complaint mechanisms did exist, they tended not to operate in an effective or timely manner taking account of children's specific circumstances. In addition to these structural issues, the research observed a lack of awareness about the impact of administrative decision-making on the lives and rights of children, with a failure to prioritise children's rights and interests implicit in the approaches taken and the decisions reached. This combined with, or was even derived from, a lack of awareness about the needs and rights of children leading to an approach that appeared to favour the process of administration over outcomes that were in children's interests. Particularly striking in this context was the absence of awareness about how quickly harm could be done to children's interests through a delay in the administrative process. Similarily regrettable was the failure to expedite decisions or proceed with special urgency where the circumstances revealed a particularly acute need. The research showed how rules or schemes were applied in an inflexible or blanket manner, regardless of their arbitrary and disproportionate effects on children's education and development, their health and well-being. Individual children appeared, in these instances, to be 'invisible in the decision-making process' (Kilkelly, 2011, p. 77) requiring carers to make continuous and exhaustive efforts to have their basic needs met. Conversely, there were specific instances where the actions of the public body amounted to a failure to implement or adhere to the requirements of national law or policy and overall, the research identified multiple instances where the administrative practices that were the subject of the complaints had led to breaches of children's rights.

The study drew an important connection between the protection of children's rights and the function of sound and fair administrative decision-making, highlighting the relationship between the different elements of the Ombudsman for Children's legislative mandate. Kilkelly's study also drew attention to the need for the Ombudsman for Children to adhere more strictly to the terms of the legislation when engaging with public bodies, as much to engender their confidence in the institution's use of power as to ensure integrity in the complaints process. The study concluded with two recommendations to the Ombudsman, first to publish more detailed guidance on the operation of its complaint functions under the legislation, with specific reference to its interpretation of the grounds of maladministration set out in section 8 of the Ombudsman for Children Act 2002, and second, to consider engaging with public bodies about their awareness of the complaints function so as to open dialogue about how the investigations function might operate better to everyone's benefit (Kilkelly, 2011). A project focused on child-friendly administration was subsequenty undertaken by the Ombudsman and the guidance on child-centred complaints, highlighted above, was an important part of this (OCO, 2018b).

## 6.6 Conclusion

This chapter has sought to shine a light on the complaint and investigation function of the Ombudsman for Children as an illustration of how such a mechanism can work both to resolve individual children's grievances while also addressing more systemic problems. The potentially demanding nature of complaint handling on the resources of an NHRI for children has been raised as a concern (Martin, 2004; Rees, 2010), highlighting how important it is that the potential of the complaints process is maximised to ensure systemic and more widespread change and reform. This is also important given that the Ombudsman for Children's recommendations are not legally binding on public bodies, something which would help to strengthen the integrity of the office if it were put in place. This might also address the passive or even active resistance to investigations experienced by the Ombudsman from some public bodies. The Ombudsman's guidance on complaints was important to improve the wider understanding of the role and purpose of the institution in this area. At the same time, there may be ambiguity to be found between the Ombudsman's assertions that a constructive and mutually agreeable resolution of the matter is the goal of the complaint mechanism and how that is received by the public body under investigation with respect to wrong-doing concerning a child. In all circumstances, rigour and fairness are essential to the integrity of the process.

There is little doubt that the range, detail and depth of concerns raised by children with the Ombudsman for Children—highlighted throughout its Annual Reports, its submissions and its special reports—continue to be a serious concern over 15 years after the institution was established. At the same time, the resolution of thousands of individual grievances and the extent to which institutional, systemic and policy matters have been highlighted and addressed stands as testament to the important work that the office does in this area. The complaint and investigation function is, as originally conceived, a cornerstone of the Ombudsman's mandate, important in its own right as a mark of the institution's independence and integrity. As the Ombudsman seeks to ensure in a variety of ways that issues raised via the complaints and investigation's function are used to wider and more long-lasting effect, it is in the integration with the institution's other more proactive powers that its authority and influence will continue to be strengthened.

## References

Charles, K. (2009). *Separated children living in Ireland*. Ombudsman for Children's Office.

Council of Europe. (2010). *Guidelines of the Committee of Ministers of the Council of Europe on child-friendly justice, adopted by the Committee of Ministers on 17 November 2010 at the 1098th meeting of the Ministers' Deputies*.

Glendenning, D. (2004). The Ombudsman for Children: An analysis of the Irish model as it relates to recognized schools. *Education and the Law, 16*(2–3), 133–143.

Kilkelly, U. (2011). *A children's rights analysis of investigations*. Ombudsman for Children's Office.

Martin, F. (2004). Key roles of the Ombudsman for Children in Ireland: Promotion of rights and investigation of grievances. *Dublin University Law Journal, 26*, 56–82.

Ombudsman for Children Act. (2002).

Ombudsman for Children. (2005). *Annual report 2005.* Ombudsman for Children's Office.

Ombudsman for Children. (2006). *Report of the Ombudsman for Children to the Oireachtas Joint Committee on Health and Children on complaints about child protection.* Ombudsman for Children's Office.

Ombudsman for Children. (2007a). *A guide to complaint handling by the Ombudsman for Children's Office.* Ombudsman for Children's Office.

Ombudsman for Children. (2007b). *Hearing children: Annual report of the Ombudsman for Children's Office January 2007-December 2007.* Ombudsman for Children's Office.

Ombudsman for Children. (2008). *Annual report 2008.* Ombudsman for Children's Office.

Ombudsman for Children. (2009a). *A guide to investigations by the Ombudsman for Children's Office.* Ombudsman for Children's Office.

Ombudsman for Children. (2009b). *Annual report 2009.* Ombudsman for Children's Office.

Ombudsman for Children. (2010). *Annual report 2010.* Ombudsman for Children's Office.

Ombudsman for Children. (2011a). *Annual report 2011.* Ombudsman for Children's Office.

Ombudsman for Children. (2011b). *A statement based on an investigation into the provision of supports and therapeutic services for a child with special needs in foster care.* Ombudsman for Children's Office.

Ombudsman for Children. (2012a). *Homeless truths: Children's experiences of homelessness in Ireland, monitoring by the Ombudsman for Children's Office of Homelessness services for children.* Ombudsman for Children's Office.

Ombudsman for Children. (2012b). *Statement on the examination and proposed investigation of HSE Homelessness Service provision to children who are homeless and accommodated under Section 5 of the Child Care Act and those in the Care of the HSE accessing homeless services.* Ombudsman for Children's Office.

Ombudsman for Children. (2012c). *A statement regarding educational provision in mainstream school for children with Down Syndrome.* Ombudsman for Children's Office.

Ombudsman for Children. (2013a). *A statement based on an investigation into provision by the Department of Education and Skills and the HSE for a child in care.* Ombudsman for Children's Office.

Ombudsman for Children. (2013b). *Report on the investigation of HSE social work service provision in North Lee.* Ombudsman for Children's Office.

Ombudsman for Children. (2016). *Annual report 2016*. Ombudsman for Children's Office.

Ombudsman for Children. (2018a). *Molly's* case: How Tusla and the HSE provided and coordinated supports for a child with a disability in the care of the state*. Ombudsman for Children's Office.

Ombudsman for Children. (2018b). *A guide to child-centred complaints handling*. Ombudsman for Children's Office.

Ombudsman for Children. (2019). *Progress for children: Annual report 2019*. Ombudsman for Children's Office.

Rees, O. (2010). Dealing with individual cases: An essential role for national human rights institutions for children? *International Journal of Children's Rights, 18*(3), 417–436.

UN Committee on the Rights of the Child. (2002, November 15). *General Comment No. 2 (2002): The role of independent national human rights institutions in the promotion and protection of the rights of the child*. CRC/GC/2002/2.

UN General Assembly. (1993). *Principles relating to the status of national institutions (Paris Principles)*. UN Doc. A/RES/48/134.

Williams, J. (2005). Effective government structures for children: The UK's four children's commissioners. *International Child and Family Law Quarterly, 17*(1), 37–53.

CHAPTER 7

# Children in Prison

**Abstract** In 2004, when the Ombudsman for Children was first established in Ireland, children aged 16 and 17 years were detained in St. Patrick's Institution, a widely criticised young offender institution. At the time, the Ombudsman for Children Act 2002 excluded children in prisons from its complaint remit and weak prison oversight, and the absence of child-centred monitoring meant that children in prison were invisible. Research for the Ombudsman for Children had identified children in the criminal justice system as an especially vulnerable group who faced multiple barriers to the realisation of their rights. Against this backdrop, the Ombudsman for Children took a strategic decision to use the broader mandate of the institution to promote the rights and welfare of children by engaging with children in St. Patrick's, to record their experiences and present them to Government to expedite proposed reforms. The Ombudsman for Children's project with children in St. Patrick's Institution illustrates how advocacy, including amplifying the voices of children themselves, can achieve change. Through this project, the Ombudsman for Children prompted others to listen to children in prison for the first time and this built the necessary momentum to close St. Patrick's, bringing an end to the imprisonment of children in Ireland.

**Keywords** Prison · Reform · Children's rights · Children's views · International support · Soft power


U. Kilkelly and E. Logan, *National Independent Human Rights Institutions for Children*,
https://doi.org/10.1007/978-3-030-80275-2_7

## 7.1 Introduction

Historically, children under 16 years were held in Ireland's Children Detention Schools, where they received care and education in line with their age and needs. Children over 16 years, by contrast, were held in adult prison, notably in St. Patrick's Institution which accommodated young people between 16 and 21 years. The Ombudsman for Children Act 2002 excluded children from prison from its complaint remit and although this exclusion had its origins in the fact that Government policy intended to transfer responsibility for all children under 18 years to the Detention Schools, the result was that in the interim, children in St. Patrick's Institution had no access to the Ombudsman.

Expressions of concern about the conditions in St. Patrick's Institution had been recorded for decades by national and international bodies. At the same time, weak prison oversight and the absence of child-centred monitoring of St. Patrick's meant that the experiences of the children themselves were largely invisible and their voices unheard. Research for the Ombudsman for Children had identified children in the criminal justice system, including children in detention, as an especially vulnerable group of children who faced multiple barriers to the realisation of their rights (Kilkelly, 2007). It was against this backdrop then that the Ombudsman for Children took a strategic decision to rely on the broader mandate of the legislation—to promote the rights and welfare of all children—to engage with children in St. Patrick's, to record their experiences and present them to Government with a view to having those rights addressed.

This chapter thus presents the Ombudsman for Children's project of engagement with children in St. Patrick's Institution as an example of the use of soft power in advocating for reform. It illustrates the contribution that the Ombudsman for Children made to bringing an end to the imprisonment of children in Ireland by using the general duty to promote the rights and welfare of children (Ombudsman for Children Act, 2002, s. 6). Using creative methodologies to enable the children to express their views and the institution's independence and credibility to ensure their voices were heard, the chapter illustrates how to effect change when the normal levers of influence are unavailable.

The chapter begins by introducing the case for reform and outlining the circumstances, including inspection and monitoring, that prevailed in relation to St. Patrick's Institution in the 2000s. It then outlines the project undertaken by the Ombudsman, documenting the views and experiences of young people of their rights, presenting both the challenges of the project and its impact.

## 7.2 St. Patrick's Institution and the Background to the Project

Ireland ratified the UN Convention on the Rights of the Child (CRC, 1989) in 1992 and around that time began a process of reforming the youth justice system, including developing a modern legislative framework. The Children Act 2001 committed to the principle that detention would be used as a measure of last resort (s. 96) and the National Youth Justice Strategy adopted in 2008 stated Government's intention to modernise and amalgamate the Children Detention Schools into a single national facility, which would take responsibility for all children up to 18 years (Irish Youth Justice Service, 2008). It was to take almost another decade before the newly established Oberstown Children Detention Campus would have responsibility for all children under 18 years, such that the doors of St. Patrick's Institution could close for the final time.

Children deprived of liberty frequently have complex and often unmet needs (Nowak, 2019) and children in St. Patrick's Institution were no different (Kilkelly, 2006). For historical reasons, while children under 16 years were detained in Children Detention Schools originally under the remit of the Department of Education and then under the Department of Children, children over 16 years were detained in adult prison under the remit of the Department of Justice. The result was a stark and indefensible difference in treatment. While progress was being made in the reform of the detention school system, to expand its remit, progress was slow (Kilkelly and Bergin, forthcoming). As a result, children over 16 years continued to be detained in St. Patrick's, a Victorian prison dating from the 1850s, with outdated accommodation, stark conditions and a poor regime that took little account of the children's needs or circumstances. Long criticised by national and international bodies including the Whitaker Committee, the Irish Penal Reform Trust (IPRT, 2007; Martynowicz & Ní Dhrisceoil, 2009) and the Council of Europe's Committee for the Prevention of Torture (CPT, 2003), it was considered 'an environment that would contribute to further delinquency of the juvenile rather than any rehabilitative function' (Walsh, 2005, p. 483).

In the first Annual Report of the Ombudsman for Children, concerns were expressed about weaknesses in the founding legislation (Ombudsman for Children [OCO], 2005) in particular, that children in prison were excluded from the institution's powers of investigation under s. 11 of the Act. At that time, approximately 60 children were detained in St. Patrick's Institution (Irish Prison Service, 2006) and the Ombudsman for Children was precluded from acting on any complaints about their detention (OCO, 2011). In 2007, research commissioned by the Ombudsman for Children highlighted that children in the criminal justice system faced multiple barriers in the realisation of their rights. It recommended that efforts be made to ensure that their voices were heard and their treatment monitored and prioritised (Kilkelly, 2007).

At the time, St. Patrick's Institution was monitored by the Prison Visiting Committee and the Inspector of Prisons. The Visiting Committee is a body whose members are appointed by Government who undertake regular visits to prisons and to which prisoners can bring complaints (Rogan, 2009), although they have no power to resolve them (Hamilton & Kilkelly, 2008). Their annual reports are submitted to the Minister for Justice. In the case of St. Patrick's, the Visiting Committee had reported little cause for concern about children's experiences arising out of its multiple unannounced visits to the prison which were designed to ensure that everything was run in an 'efficient, fair, safe and humanitarian way' (St. Patrick's Institution Visiting Committee, 2007, p. 1). This, the Committee was 'pleased to confirm has always been the case' (St. Patrick's Institution Visiting Committee, 2007, p. 1). The Committee consistently reported many positive developments in St. Patrick's, such as the advancement in education opportunities, new security measures and improvements in visiting arrangements and in 2007 concluded that:

> As in previous years, we wish to place on record that from our observations, in this institution the welfare of the inmates is of primary concern. The Committee wish to record our thanks and appreciation to the Governor and his staff for the excellent management and running of the institution. (St. Patrick's Institution Prison Visiting Committee 2007, p. 1)

Although it is not clear whether the Committee met with the 'inmates' the 2007 report does say that 'representations which we have made on behalf of inmates are being considered and where possible and practical are being addressed by prison management' (St. Patrick's Institution

Visiting Committee, 2007, p. 4). The Committee expressed concern in 2008 that they had so few requests to meet with them and they took measures to raise awareness about their role (St. Patrick's Institution Visiting Committee, 2008). Regardless, the huge disparity between the reports of the Committee and the findings of the Ombudsman for Children set out below, clearly highlights that the Visiting Committee, as established, did not take direct account of the experiences and views of young people detained in St. Patrick's.

Following several years as a non-statutory body, the Inspector of Prisons was established under the Prisons Act 2007, with powers (s. 31) to undertake regular inspections of prisons at any time, but not to investigate or adjudicate on individual prisoner complaints. The 2006–2007 report of Justice Kinlen, then Inspector of Prisons, had openly acknowledged that the regime in which young people were detained in St. Patrick's Institution was very poor with no individualised education or care plans, skeletal mental health services and serious problems with bullying and drugs (Inspector of Prisons, 2007). Judge Michael Reilly, appointed as the first statutory Inspector of Prisons in 2008, published human rights-based standards for the inspection of prisons, with a juvenile supplement that year. However, the Inspector's Annual Report 2008 made little reference to the conditions or regime of detention in St. Patrick's, highlighting instead the importance of expediting the development of the Oberstown child detention facility which, it was intended, would take responsibility for all children under 18 years (Inspector of Prisons, 2009a). The Inspector's report in 2009–2010 also dealt with the facility in brief, although it did observe that 'prisoners on protection are a significant problem. Numbers of juveniles and young adults spend much of their time in their cells even if not on protection' (Inspector of Prisons, 2011, p. 12).

## 7.3 The Ombudsman for Children's Project

These circumstances—concerns about children's experiences of detention in St. Patrick's and the invisibility of these experiences from prison monitoring—prompted the Ombudsman for Children to take a strategic decision to engage with children in St. Patrick's Institution about their experiences of their rights. Deprived of the Ombudsman's complaint and investigation function, recourse was had instead to the powers set out under section 7 of the Ombudsman for Children Act 2002 to consult with children, highlight children's rights issues that are of concern to them, advise Ministers on matters relating to the rights and welfare of children, and encourage public bodies to develop policies, practices and procedures that promote the rights and welfare of children. The project was thus specifically designed to hear directly from children about their experiences of their rights in St. Patrick's Institution, to present these views to the authorities who would be given the opportunity to formally respond, in order to provide a much needed, children's rights perspective to the reform of their detention in Ireland.

### 7.3.1 *Beginning the Project, Building Trust*

The first formal phase of the project was a literature review of the relevant national and international standards in relation to children in detention, drawing on a study by the Irish Penal Reform Trust (Martynowicz & Ní Dhrisceoil, 2009). A significant number of preparatory meetings took place between the Ombudsman for Children's team and key stakeholders and sustained preparatory dialogue with the prison authorities took place prior to the commencement of the project. Discussions also took place with the children prior to the formal commencement of the project and during the course of those meetings, a number of priorities emerged. The first was the realisation that the sessions with the young people needed to take place without the supervision of prison officers, and the second was that trust needed to be built with the young people, who needed an assurance of confidentiality before they would express their views (OCO, 2011). This prompted the Ombudsman's team to take advice on how to build the trust on which the project depended. With the assistance of a homeless charity, engagement took place between the Ombudsman for Children team and a group of young men living in inner-city Dublin, all of whom had been detained in St. Patrick's Institution at one point (OCO, 2011). This process enabled the Ombudsman to hear from those with direct experience of St. Patrick's, who provided invaluable advice on how trust might be built with the young people such as to enable them to have the confidence to participate safely in the project.

### 7.3.2 *Approach to the Participation of the Children and Young People*

The circumstances of the young people, including poor literacy and complex needs, meant that the consultation needed to be carefully and sensitively planned (OCO, 2011). The team met with the young people on several occasions over a two-month period ahead of the start of the project, which lasted three months, providing an informal opportunity to develop trust and relationships and to explain the background to and purpose of the project.

Two complementary methodologies were used. The first involved a series of focus group interviews with young people based around specific themes, which were benchmarked against national and international standards on the detention of children. The young people identified the themes for the consultation and agreed to work together in small groups, in regular two-hour sessions. The second and complementary method involved art sessions, led by an art teacher with an external facilitator. This had the significant benefit of providing powerful ways for the young people to communicate their experiences safely, without inhibition (OCO, 2011). Their views and experiences, recorded in the interviews and their drawings, formed the basis not only for the Ombudsman for Children's report to parliament, but also for an animated short film, presenting the experience of young people in their own words using their art. Consideration was given to releasing the material into mainstream media, with a decision taken to not sanitise the film or report to ensure the voices of the young people remained authentic.

## 7.4 The Findings of the Consultation

This next section presents the findings from the consultation with the young people, with each section prefaced by a short summary of the relevant international standards set out in the Havana Rules (1990) and the European Rules for Juveniles subject to Sanctions and Measures (Council of Europe, 2008).

### *7.4.1 Committal, Orientation and Sentence Planning*

International standards provide that on admission to detention, young people must be given a copy of the rules and have a written description of their rights and obligations in a form they can understand. Each young person should be interviewed and a psychological and social report, identifying any factors relevant to their care, should be prepared. National standards provide that a sentence plan should be drawn up for each young person as soon as possible after their committal, with the views of the young person given due consideration in the development of the plan, which should be multidisciplinary in nature, and aim to address the young person's offending behaviour, and prepare him for release (Inspector of Prisons, 2009b).

The experience of the young people in St. Patrick's was varied. Some reported situations where they received no or very little information about the rules of the institution—'*we don't know what the rules are…we don't know what we are entitled to*' (OCO, 2011, p. 23). Most young people said that on first committal, they relied heavily on informal communications with their peers and on their own observations to find out how things work and about any programmes or services available:

> *… you'd find out off someone out in the yard or you'd learn it yourself.*
> *… for the first good few weeks I was in, I was just down in the gym every day, because I didn't have a clue how to get classes … And I just copped on after a while and went up for an interview then.* (OCO, 2011, p. 23)

As to how this might be improved, several young people thought written information would be helpful: '*It'd be handy … At least they'd know they're getting up at a certain time, and … when they're going back to their cells*' (OCO, 2011, p. 23). But they were clear that young people who had poor literacy would have problems understanding such information and suggested instead, that a one-to-one session with a member of staff following committal, where practical information could be communicated to the young person, would be very helpful. They described meetings with the deputy governor, with probation service staff and their medical assessment team, but did not experience or perceive them to be part of an individualised care or sentence plan. The young people had no sense that their views mattered or were seriously considered in the context of sentence planning (OCO, 2011).

### *7.4.2 Separation from Adults*

The CRC is clear that every child deprived of their liberty is to be separated from adults unless it is in their interests not to do so, and the CRC Committee (2019, para. 92) has stressed that separate facilities should be staffed by appropriately trained personnel, that operate according to child-friendly policies and practices.

In St. Patrick's, the young people advised that the application of these rules was, at the very least, inconsistent. For a variety of reasons, young people were detained on the same landings as adults because the old building environment presented challenges separating them from adults (OCO, 2011). Apart from one wing which they thought was unsafe, the young people mainly viewed the way in which activities were organised for adults as impeding *their* ability to be actively involved: '*School is grand ... but we should be able to go round to the workshops ... Every other wing gets ... the school workshops ... there's metalwork ... woodwork, industrial skills ... You can make a lot more stuff, and sign out a lot more stuff ... there's much better equipment down there than anywhere else*' (OCO, 2011, p. 26).

### *7.4.3 Accommodation*

International standards are clear that young people need accommodation that is in keeping with the rehabilitative aims of residential placements (CRC Committee, 2019, para. 89). In St. Patrick's, the young people spoke in some detail about living standards in prison and it was clear that the environment had a considerable impact on both their experience of detention and the extent to which their dignity and worth are respected (OCO, 2011). Their cells were clearly of most significance to them:

> *There's a bed, there's a telly. There's a mattress that's ... like a duvet cover. ... The mattress is that skinny, you're able to fold it into a little ball ... You're sleeping on a lump of steel ... You can feel everything on your back ... It's just like a concrete block. ... There's a counter beside the bed. A little metal counter. Stuck to the wall ... And two little lockers ... You'd fit ... a t-shirt and a pair of bottoms and a pair of jocks and socks in this thing. ... Then there's a shelf with your telly on it. And then there's a toilet.* (OCO, 2011, p. 29)

They criticised the security of personal property, poor ventilation, the discomfort of the beds and the condition of the bed sheets. A number spoke about the psychological impact of these conditions, with one young person saying: 'we're going off our heads in the cells' (OCO, 2011, p. 30). They were responsible for keeping their cells clean, and while they were glad of in-cell sanitation, they were anxious about the lack of privacy, knowing that in practice prison officers could open the hatch door at any stage (OCO, 2011). They were enthusiastic with suggestions for improvements, which ranged from better quality cleaning products for cells, to clothing and privacy.

### 7.4.4 *Health*

Article 24 of the CRC states that all children have the right to the enjoyment of the highest attainable standard of health and states shall strive to ensure that no child is deprived of their right to access to health care services.

The young people in St. Patrick's spoke about several issues relating to their physical and mental health, including access to health professionals; alcohol and drug cessation programmes and counselling services; treatment of illness and accidents; food and access to clean drinking water (OCO, 2011). Not unusual for young people of their age, they were reticent to talk about mental health, but they did communicate that when they did speak up or openly with prison authorities about 'finding it hard' this usually resulted in them being placed 'on protection' or putting them in 'the pad' or special observation cell:

> *…you could talk to the Governor, but that means you'd be going on protection…just get locked up for 23 hours a day.*
>
> *… if you went down there and you said to one of the counsellors 'I'm suicidal, I'm thinking of killing myself' … they stick you in the pad, do you know what I mean? That's why you don't … You don't open your mouth about anything like that … You don't open your mouth.* (OCO, 2011, p. 36)

### 7.4.5 *Education, Training and Recreation*

The Global Study on Children Deprived of Liberty outlines the importance of childhood as a time when children develop their personality, their emotional relationships with others and their social and educational skills (Nowak, 2019). In the Study, children themselves talked about the importance to them of education, a right given international protection in Articles 28 and 29 of the CRC. In St. Patrick's, the young people liked that the decision to attend school was theirs. For those who chose to participate in education, their principal motivations were that it was '*better than being in the cell*' and that it presented the opportunity to develop skills (OCO, 2011, p. 42). The programmes available included accredited courses that would allow preparation for state exams, although this was taken up by very few. Focus on literacy or reading illustrated their poor level of education. The content of the other programmes was largely vocational in nature, covering woodwork, arts and crafts and cooking.

Many of the young people expressed disappointment with the range of education and training options. They were interested in accessing skills-based and trade-oriented opportunities that would ultimately help them to secure employment on release, citing metalwork, mechanics, industrial skills, IT and technical drawing as areas of interest (OCO, 2011, p. 42). While their aspiration for state exams was low, this seemed to have been influenced by the similarly poor aspirations held by staff.

### *7.4.6 Contact with Family and Community*

Article 37 of the CRC recognises the right of every child deprived of liberty to maintain contact with their families through correspondence and visits. To facilitate visits, the child should be placed in a facility as close as possible to their family's place of residence, exceptions that may limit contact should be clearly described in law and not left to the discretion of authorities (CRC Committee, 2019, para. 94).

The issue of contact with family and how it was facilitated, or not, was the theme of most significance to the children and young people. At the time, children who were sentenced were allowed two half-hour visits per week and children on remand were allowed up to five fifteen-minute visits per week, while all were allowed a six-minute daily phone call (OCO, 2011). In their experience, the visits were usually 'screened', which precluded them from any physical contact in an effort to combat the flow of drugs into the prison (OCO, 2011, p. 46). In practice, this meant that they had to raise their voices to be heard, embarrassed that everyone would hear their conversation, including prison officers.

> *There is a big screen in the way ... you've all people roaring trying to hear ... You can't hear nothing ... You're trying to hear something and you can't hear. You spend most of your visit saying 'What?'*
>
> *... screen visits with an officer sitting there, close enough to you ... and they can hear what you're saying ... there's no real privacy.* (OCO, 2011, p. 47)

Other exceptional 'special visits' existed but were not seen as a viable option by young people because it impinged on their privacy, with a prison officer in attendance. They were aware that their letters were read and so did not see the point of writing to or receiving letters from family. Poor literacy levels posed further barriers to communication. In general, the young people experienced decisions about family contact and visits as a mechanism of control and punishment of behaviour.

### 7.4.7 *Safety, Protection and Disciplinary Measures*

Taken together, Articles 19 and 37 of the CRC oblige states parties to take all appropriate measures to protect children from all forms of violence and to ensure that every child in detention should be treated with respect for their inherent dignity (CRC Committee, 2019, paras. 92–95).

The young people in St. Patrick's were resigned to the very fact that being in a prison environment offered no expectation of safety (OCO, 2011, p. 53) saying: '*It's a prison … You can't seem to feel safe in a prison.*'

There were reports of restraint, inappropriate use of force, peer bullying and violence. They described their reticence about seeking support for peer bullying given that any approach to staff resulted in being branded a '*rat*' (OCO, 2011, p. 53). They were able to nominate individuals or groups of staff that could be trusted, this included teachers, drug counsellors, probation staff and chaplains but while a small number commented favourably on certain individuals, overall, the young people had a negative view of prison officers. They felt that some had very little respect for them, noted that their cells were left in poor condition after searches, they experienced threatening behaviour and a small number sometimes felt unsafe in their cells (OCO, 2011). Amidst a generally poor approach to safety and protection, the two most concerning practices were a lack of reporting of child protection breaches and the arbitrary use of a 'special observation cell'. The approach to child protection stemmed largely from a lack of acceptance by authorities that these young people were children, and the use of the special observation cell left young people fearful and anxious, threatened by its use and degraded by the practice of being left in a dirty cell in a pair of underpants.

### 7.4.8 *Complaints and Inspections*

The CRC Committee emphasises that every child should have the right to make requests or complaints, without censorship as to the substance, to the central administration, the judicial authority or any other proper independent authority, and to be informed of the response without delay (2019, para. 95). Children need to know their rights and to know about and have easy access to complaint mechanisms. In addition, independent and qualified inspectors should be empowered to conduct inspections on a regular basis and to undertake unannounced inspections on their own initiative: they should place special emphasis on holding conversations with children in the facilities, in a confidential setting.

In St. Patrick's, while the young people were aware of the Inspector of Prisons and the Prison Visiting Committee, they had little to say by way of comment other than querying whether it could contribute to improving the conditions and situations they experienced during their detention (OCO, 2011). They indicated that there was a visible effort by the prison to communicate about the complaint mechanism which started during the period of this work by the Ombudsman for Children.

> *... they're after sticking up a load of signs around the jail ... if you want to put in a complaint, do this and do that.*
>
> *... the last week or something, they started putting round little sheets saying ... [they] take complaints very seriously and ... how to get a complaint form.* (OCO, 2011, p. 59)

All of the young people were sceptical about bringing a complaint against a member of staff (OCO, 2011). Their key concerns centred on whether they would be believed and whether the complaint would or could be handled impartially. On the question of being believed, several young people suggested that a young person bringing a complaint should be able to call other young people as witnesses and that due weight should be given to the accounts of witnesses, the question was of course, whether the witnesses would also not be believed:

> *... you can call a witness but there's fucking no point calling a witness because .... [they] won't believe them either ... And they never listen to you when you say 'I want to call a witness'.* (OCO, 2011, p. 60)

Their doubts about the impartiality of the complaint process went beyond internal mechanisms to include existing external oversight bodies. A number of the young people said they would navigate this dilemma by making complaints informally and anonymously through the chaplains:

> *The best person would be the nuns [the chaplains]. They keep your name quiet and they do something about it.* (OCO, 2011, p. 60)

Referring to the difficulties of bringing a complaint, one young person suggested that there was a need for an independent, external mechanism to deal with complaints:

> *They have one [an ombudsman] for the Garda and they have one for children, like. They should have one for prisoners as well.* (OCO, 2011, p. 60)

## 7.5 Reaction and Response

The experiences of children in St. Patrick's, documented by the Ombudsman for Children, stood in stark contrast to the reports of the other bodies that visited around the same time. Efforts to undermine the Ombudsman's process began almost straight away and in a tacit reference to the Ombudsman's findings, the Inspector of Prisons noted as follows in a report to the Minister for Justice:

> Uncorroborated statements which have assumed the authority of anecdotal evidence suggest that prisoners and juveniles in particular were unsafe in St. Patrick's Institution. During all of my inspections I have not found evidence to support this assertion. (Inspector of Prisons, 2010, para. 17.21)

However, following the publication of the Ombudsman for Children's report in 2011, the attention paid by inspection bodies to children's treatment in St. Patrick's was to change demonstrably. In addition to the response from the Prison Service to young people's experiences of their rights (which was incorporated in the publication itself), a number of meetings were held between the Ombudsman and Government officials, including the Minister for Justice to discuss the concerns. In 2012, the Inspector of Prisons published a report dedicated to St. Patrick's Institution (Inspector of Prisons, 2012) with two striking elements. First, in contrast to the earlier statement, the report confirmed the findings published in the Ombudsman for Children's report (Inspector of Prisons, 2012). Second, this was made possible because of a change in practice when, for the first time, the Inspector met with the young people to hear about their lived experiences, a practice that emerged from his discussions with the Ombudsman for Children. As a result, the inspection process was qualitatively different than previous approaches where instead of being referred to as 'inmates', the Inspector's report frames the report from the children's perspective, referring to them liberally throughout. This represented a significant shift in culture and approach to independent monitoring of children in detention at the national level. The approach of the Ombudsman for Children had had an impact.

## 7.6 Engaging International Support

In order to strengthen the voices of the young people further, and to counter efforts at a national level to undermine or ignore the Ombudsman's report, support was sought from regional and international monitoring bodies with responsibility for the rights of children in detention. Over a period of five years, the UN Committee on the Rights of the Child, the Council of Europe Committee for the Prevention of Torture (CPT), the UN Committee Against Torture (CAT) and the Council of Europe's Commissioner for Human Rights all supported the Ombudsman for Children's call for an extended mandate to allow children and young people in St. Patrick's access to the institution. In 2006, for instance, the CRC Committee (2006, para. 72) expressed its deep concern that children continued to be detained in St. Patrick's and were without the complaint mandate of the Ombudsman for Children. The Committee (2006, para. 73) recommended that the state party include all places of detention where children are held to be included in the Ombudsman for Children investigatory mandate . It also recommended that the state party, together with the Ombudsman for Children, review and propose amendments to the specific provisions which limit the scope of the investigative powers with a view to eliminating possible gaps which may result in a violation of children's rights (CRC Committee, 2006, para. 14).

A country visit by the CPT, a year later, also recommended that the Ombudsman for Children be permitted access to prison institutions to meet with children, to raise any concerns relating to their conditions of detention and treatment, something on which the CPT requested Government to confirm had taken place subsequently (CPT, 2007, para. 100). In 2008, this call was reiterated by the Council of Europe's Commissioner for Human Rights, Thomas Hammarberg, following his country visit to Ireland (Commissioner for Human Rights, 2008, para. 17).

Ireland's first periodic review and constructive dialogue with the UN Committee against Torture (CAT) was also timely (Irish Council for Civil Liberties and Irish Penal Reform Trust, 2011). The Ombudsman for Children, although not in attendance at the hearing, made the report on St. Patrick's available to the Committee and it had also been referenced in the NGO submissions (Irish Council for Civil Liberties and Irish Penal Reform Trust, 2011). Citing the Ombudsman for Children's report and the views and experience of the children in St. Patrick's, the Committee challenged Government about the treatment of children in St. Patrick's and the lack of access for children to an independent complaint mechanism, specifically the Ombudsman for Children (CAT, 2011).

However, in the course of this dialogue with the Committee a senior civil servant reported that the St. Patrick's report merely documented the views of a selection of offenders and that 'in doing so the report identified a number of discrepancies between the young people's perception and the actual reality' (McDonald, 2011). This approach was later criticised by the Ombudsman for Children as misrepresenting the work of her institution before a UN Committee and reflected a persistent culture that suggested that young people's views could be dismissed (McDonald, 2011).

The CAT (2011, para. 22) expressed that it was 'gravely concerned' about the continued detention of young people in St. Patrick's, emphasising that it was a custodial rather than a care facility designed for children. The Committee expressed 'deep concern' that the Ombudsman for Children had no mandate to investigate allegations of acts in violation of the Convention there, leaving children in St. Patrick's without access to an external complaint mechanism. The Committee recommended that the state review its legislation with a view to including in the Ombudsman's mandate the power to investigate complaints of torture and ill-treatment of children held at St. Patricks Institution (CAT, 2011, para. 23).

## 7.7 Conclusion

On 22 June 2012, the Minister for Children and the Minister for Justice signed a ministerial order removing the provision from the Ombudsman for Children Act 2002 which excluded children detained in St. Patrick's Institution from the complaint remit of the Ombudsman for Children. This followed on from the announcement by the Minister for Children that the process of detaining children in St. Patrick's would end within two years, with no new committals of 16-year-olds to the Institution from May 2012. In fact, it was to take until 2017 before the responsibility for all children under 18 years transferred to Oberstown Children Detention Campus, with the closure of St. Patrick's Institution. But for the five years from 2012 to 2017, children in detention, regardless of whether they were detained in adult or children's facilities, could make complains to the Ombudsman for Children.

The Government had made the decision that all children under 18 years were to be detained in a specialist child detention facility long before the Ombudsman for Children published the report on the engagement with young people in St. Patrick's Institution in 2011. What was clear, however, was that while progress was being made to prepare the Children Detention Schools to take responsibility from the prisons for 16- and 17-year-olds, little attention was being paid to those children who continued to be detained in unacceptably poor conditions in St. Patrick's. The intervention of the Ombudsman for Children in this area thus shone an important light on these children's experiences of their rights, reminding authorities that they too had a voice that deserved to be heard. Doing so without the statutory mandate to investigate their complaints was an important reminder of the importance of soft power—especially where it emanated from young people themselves—in advocating for children's rights.

The Ombudsman for Children's engagement with young people in St. Patrick's led in the short term to the extension of the office's complaint mandate to children in prison. It also demonstrated to those who had the statutory remit to inspect the prison, the importance of speaking directly to children themselves about their experiences. It was in this way too an exemplar of the leadership role that must be played by the national human rights institution for children and the strategic and sustainable benefits of such an approach. The Ombudsman's role in enabling young people in St. Patrick's to find their voice also took determination in the face of antipathy and resistance. Relationships with civil society helped to leverage international treaty bodies who added pressure on the Government to respond.

Ultimately, the work of the Ombudsman in this area will be remembered not only for listening to young people in St. Patrick's, but for ensuring that those in authority heard what they had to say. In this way, the office played an influential role in finally bringing to an end the detention of children in adult prisons in Ireland, a process completed without the usual powers of investigation. In all of these ways, this case study is an exemplar of how such reform can be achieved.

## References

Children Act. (2001).

Commissioner for Human Rights. (2008). *Report by the Commissioner for Human Rights, Mr. Thomas Hammarberg, on his visit to Ireland 26–30 November 2007*. CommDH (2008) 9.

Council of Europe: Committee for the Prevention of Torture (CPT). (2003, September 18). *Report to the Government of Ireland on the visit to Ireland carried out by the European committee for the prevention of torture and inhuman or degrading treatment or punishment (CPT) from 20 to 28 May 2002*. CPT/Inf (2003) 36.

Council of Europe: Committee for the Prevention of Torture (CPT). (2007, October 10). *Report to the Government of Ireland on the visit to Ireland carried out by the European committee for the prevention of torture and inhuman or degrading treatment or punishment (CPT) from 2 to 13 October 2006*. CPT/Inf (2007) 40.

Council of Europe: Committee of Ministers. (2008, November 5). *Recommendation CM/Rec(2008)11 of the Committee of Ministers to member states on the European Rules for juvenile offenders subject to sanctions or measures*. CM/Rec(2008)11.

Hamilton, C., & Kilkelly, U. (2008). Human rights in Irish prisons. *Judicial Studies Institute Journal, 2*, 58–85.

Inspector of Prisons. (2007). *Fifth annual report of the Inspector of Prisons and places of detention for the year 2006–2007*. http://www.justice.ie/en/JELR/annualreport2007pdf.pdf/Files/annualreport2007pdf.pdf. Accessed 15 Apr 2021.

Inspector of Prisons. (2009a). *Office of the Inspector of Prisons annual report 2008*. Inspector of Prisons.

Inspector of Prisons. (2009b). *Standards for the inspection of prisons in Ireland*. Inspector of Prisons.

Inspector of Prisons. (2010). *The Irish prison population—An examination of duties and obligations owed to prisoners*. Inspector of Prisons.

Inspector of Prisons. (2011). *Annual report 2010*. Inspector of Prisons.

Inspector of Prisons. (2012). *Report on an inspection of St. Patrick's Institution by the Inspector of Prisons Judge Michael Reilly*. Inspector of Prisons.

Irish Council for Civil Liberties and Irish Penal Reform Trust. (2011). *Joint Shadow Report to the First Periodic Review of Ireland under the United Nations*

*Convention against Torture and Other Cruel, Inhuman or Degrading Treatment or Punishment*. Irish Council for Civil Liberties and Irish Penal Reform Trust.

Irish Penal Reform Trust (IPRT). (2007). *The Whitaker Committee report 20 years on: Lessons learned or lessons forgotten?* IPRT.

Irish Prison Service. (2006). *Annual report 2004*. Irish Prison Service.

Irish Youth Justice Service. (2008). *National youth justice strategy 2008–2010*. Stationery Office.

Kilkelly, U. (2006). *Youth justice in Ireland*. Irish Academic Press.

Kilkelly, U. (2007). *Barriers to the realisation of children's rights in Ireland*. Ombudsman for Children's Office.

Kilkelly, U., & Bergin, P. (2022, forthcoming). *Advancing children's rights in detention: An international model for reform*. Policy Press.

Martynowicz, A., & Ní Dhrisceoil, V. (2009). *Detention of children in Ireland: International standards and best practice*. Irish Penal Reform Trust.

McDonald, D. (2011, June 2). Children's watchdog hits out at top aide's comments. *Independent*. Available at: https://www.independent.ie/irish-news/childrens-watchdog-hits-out-at-top-aides-comments-26738555.html. Accessed 15 Apr 2021.

Nowak, M. (2019). *The United Nations global study on children deprived of liberty*. UN.

Ombudsman for Children Act. (2002).

Ombudsman for Children. (2005). *Annual report 2005*. Ombudsman for Children's Office.

Ombudsman for Children. (2011). *Young people in St. Patrick's Institution—A report by the Ombudsman for Children's Office*. Ombudsman for Children's Office.

Prisons Act. (2007).

Rogan, M. (2009). Visiting committees and accountability in the Irish prison system: Some proposals for reform. *Dublin University Law Journal, 31*, 298–323.

St. Patrick's Institution Visiting Committee. (2007). *Annual report for year ending 31st December 2007*. http://www.justice.ie/en/JELR/St.Patricks%20VC%20Annual%20Report%202007.pdf/Files/St.Patricks%20VC%20Annual%20Report%202007.pdf. Accessed 1 Apr 2021.

St. Patrick's Institution Prison Visiting Committee. (2008). *Annual report for year ending 31st December 2008*. Available at: http://www.justice.ie/en/JELR/StPatricks%202008.pdf/Files/StPatricks%202008.pdf. Accessed 1 Apr 2021.

UN Committee against Torture (CAT). (2011). *Consideration of reports submitted by States parties under article 19 of the Convention, concluding observations: Ireland*, Forty-sixth session, 9 May–3 June 2011, CAT/C/IRL/CO/1.

UN Committee on the Rights of the Child. (2006, September 29). *Concluding observations: Ireland*. CRC/C/IRL/CO/2.
UN Committee on the Rights of the Child. (2019, September 18). *General Comment No. 24 (2019) on children's rights in the child justice system.* CRC/C/GC/24.
UN Convention on the Rights of the Child (CRC). (1989).
United Nations Rules for the Protection of Juveniles Deprived of their Liberty (The Havana Rules). (1990). *Adopted by General Assembly resolution 45/113 of 14 December 1990.*
Walsh, D. P. J. (2005). *Juvenile justice.* Thomson Round Hall.

CHAPTER 8

# Separated Children Seeking International Protection

**Abstract** Migration poses significant risks to children's rights which are exacerbated when children are separated from their family or care givers. Research for the Ombudsman for Children identified that asylum seeker and refugee children face multiple barriers to the enjoyment of their rights, noting that separated children seeking international protection, who are without family care, are considered additionally vulnerable. Concern about the rights of separated children, who were excluded from the complaint remit of Ombudsman for Children, led to a strategic decision to undertake a nine-month consultation with them about their rights. Using creative methodologies, the Ombudsman for Children helped separated children to document their concerns about their treatment, bringing their views and experiences together in a report used to bring about reform in their care, accommodation and protection by the state. The project was an important example of how the Ombudsman for Children can fulfil the duty to promote and protect children's rights by ensuring that the voices of a vulnerable group of children were heard so that reforms were secured, and awareness raised about their rights among children, decision-makers and the public.

**Keywords** Separated children · International protection · Reform · Consultation with children · Creativity · Advocacy



U. Kilkelly and E. Logan, *National Independent Human Rights Institutions for Children*,
https://doi.org/10.1007/978-3-030-80275-2_8

## 8.1 Introduction

At the end of 2019, the UN High Commissioner for Refugees (UNHCR) reported that an estimated 79.5 million persons were forcibly displaced worldwide, with an estimated 30–34 million children (UNHCR, 2019). Among these are an estimated 138,600 unaccompanied and separated children, a figure that UNHCR reports as being a significant underestimate (UNHCR, 2018). Refugee children face significant risks to their rights, and these are exacerbated further for children deprived of family care, separated from parents or caregivers. The United Nations Convention on the Rights of the Child (CRC, 1989) sets out the rights to which all children are entitled and according to the Committee on the Rights of the Child, there should be no discrimination on the basis of a child's status as a refugee, whether separated or unaccompanied (CRC Committee, 2005, para. 18). While the refugee child has a right to special protection, care and assistance under Article 22 of the CRC, the CRC Committee has recognised the particular vulnerability of separated children seeking international protection who face multifaceted challenges to the enjoyment of their rights (CRC Committee, 2005, para. 8). Problems include the absence of guardianship, accommodation and interim care, access to education, and problems with family tracing, reunification, settlement and integration (Keogh & Whyte, 2003). On arrival in a new country, separated children often have to cope with loss of loved ones, the challenges of an entirely new culture and the associated threat to their sense of identity (Ní Raghallaigh & Gilligan, 2010). They have to deal with uncertainty about their futures and the stresses associated with the asylum process (Ní Raghallaigh & Gilligan, 2010). Against this backdrop, there are a range of negative and positive obligations on state authorities to ensure the rights of separated children are adequately protected (CRC Committee, 2005, para. 13). The Committee has noted that when properly understood, non-discrimination may require differentiation on the basis of separated children's different protection needs (CRC Committee, 2005, para. 18), making it clear that this requires very particular attention.

Ireland's system of international protection developed quickly in the 1990s. By the early 2000s, hundreds of children were arriving into Ireland every year without parental care. These children were referred to a relatively ad hoc system of care and protection, from which many children 'disappeared' (Ombudsman for Children [OCO], 2006a). In 2007, research for the Ombudsman for Children identified that separated children seeking asylum were at grave risk of breaches of their rights to protection from harm, including trafficking; from racism and discrimination; and from poverty (Kilkelly, 2007, p. 31). Doubly discriminated against because of their status as children and as asylum seekers, separated children were found to be largely invisible within the system (Kilkelly, 2007, p. 35).

Reflecting the gravity of these concerns, the Ombudsman for Children took a strategic decision in 2009 to consult separated children about their experiences and, relying on the institution's statutory duty to promote and protect children's rights, sought to successfully advocate for reform of their care and treatment in line with international standards of protection. The aim of this chapter therefore is to illustrate the Ombudsman for Children's Separated Children project, where creative methodologies were used to enable separated children to talk about their rights, to enable the institution to advocate for reform in their treatment by the state.

The chapter begins with an introduction to Ireland's system of international protection before detailing the Ombudsman for Children's Separated Children project, setting out its findings and impacts.

## 8.2 Separated Children in Ireland

Although historically a country of significant emigration (Arnold et al., 2018, p. 16), since the 1990s Ireland has been a country of 'net immigration' (Crowley et al., 2008, p. 141), forcing rapid development of the relevant legislative and policy framework (Ruhs & Quinn, 2009). By 1998, the CRC Committee had specifically raised with Ireland its concern about the implementation of Article 2 with respect to the difficulties faced by children from vulnerable and disadvantaged groups, including refugee children (CRC Committee, 1998, para. 14). In the 2000s, separated children who entered Ireland were placed in the care of the Health Service Executive (HSE), which at the time had legislative responsibility for their care under Ireland's child protection and refugee laws. The HSE's Separated Children Seeking Asylum (SCSA) service was primarily responsible for the delivery of services to separated children, with duties to provide for their immediate and ongoing care; social, medical and psychological services; liaison with educational and youth services; tracing relatives; and providing assessments and reunification where safe and possible (Charles, 2009, p. 14).

In 2004, the SCSA service reported that 630 separated children arrived in Ireland and over 600 arrived in 2005 (OCO, 2006a, p. 45). The numbers of separated children in Ireland peaked to 1372 in 2007 (HSE, 2008a, p. 28). Not long after the establishment of the Ombudsman for Children, the institution began to express concern, nationally and internationally, about the unequal treatment of separated children, in contravention of Article 2 of the CRC (OCO, 2005; O'Brien, 2007). In 2008, the HSE reported in a review of the adequacy of its children and family services that separated children were 'going missing', noting that 7% of separated children were unaccounted for that year (HSE, 2008a, p. 41). At the time, over half of the separated children were reported as having been reunited with family members in the state (OCO, 2006a, p. 45) and the remainder were placed in residential centres in Dublin and throughout the country (OCO, 2006a, p. 45).

Taking account of these international standards and concerns about the treatment of separated children in Ireland, the Ombudsman for Children decided to visit a number of centres for separated children and reported to the CRC Committee in 2006 that the vast majority of separated children were accommodated in 'hostel' accommodation (OCO, 2006a, p. 46). The hostels were privately owned and run and operated by staff who, in the main, were not childcare professionals, in stark contrast to the conditions in which Irish children in state care were accommodated (OCO, 2006a). Among other concerns, the Ombudsman for Children reported the inferior care provided to separated children, the lack of initiatives to facilitate their participation in the centres and the lack of access to an independent guardian or adviser (OCO, 2006a). A particularly acute concern, at that time, was the risk such children faced of being trafficked (CRC Committee, 2005, para. 50; O'Brien, 2007).

In advance of Ireland's second periodic report to the CRC Committee, the Ombudsman for Children wrote to the Chair of the UN Committee on the Rights of the Child inviting the Committee to visit (OCO, 2006b, p. 23). The main purpose of the three-day visit was to co-ordinate meetings between the members of the Committee and children, including a group of separated children, to hear directly about their experiences of their rights (*The Irish Times*, 2006). In its Concluding Observations, issued following its consideration of Ireland's second periodic report, the Committee emphasised its concern for unaccompanied and separated children, expressing concern that children separated from their parents might not receive adequate guidance, support and protection during the asylum process, in particular with respect to access to services and independent representation (CRC Committee, 2006, para. 64). The Committee recommended that the state party ensure that the same standards of and access to support services applies whether the child is in the care of authorities or their parents, drawing attention to General Comment No. 6 on the treatment of unaccompanied and separated children outside their country of origin (CRC Committee, 2006, para. 65).

## 8.3 The Ombudsman for Children's Project

In its General Comment No. 2, the CRC Committee (2002) recommended that in the spirit of Article 2, National Human Rights Institutions (NHRIs) for children should proactively reach out to all groups of children, in particular the most vulnerable and disadvantaged, such as children in care or detention, refugee and migrant children and other groups. The Committee recommended that such institutions should have the right of access, in conditions of privacy, to children in all forms of alternative care or other places (CRC Committee, 2002, para. 15). The Committee also recommended that NHRIs for children should 'devise specially tailored consultation programmes and imaginative communication strategies to ensure full compliance with Article 12 of the Convention' (CRC Committee, 2002, para. 17).

Consistent with this guidance and taking account of the fact that the Ombudsman for Children did not appear to have the mandate to receive complaints from separated children (OCO, 2006a, pp. 14–15), the institution sought instead to use its broader power (under s. 7 of the Ombudsman for Children Act, 2002) to promote the rights of children, conducting research and consulting with children to document their experiences of their rights. In line with the Act, the Ombudsman already had a structure in place to consult with children but on review, its Youth Advisory Panel was not considered representative of separated children living in Ireland. Accordingly, a second youth advisory panel was established including two young people, Leylah and Ahmed, who were separated children living in state care (Charles, 2009, p. 11). They formed part of the team involved in early preparations and discussions about how to engage with the young people in a way that they would enjoy, including during their summer holidays (Charles, 2009, p. 18).

At an early stage of engaging with children in the project, it became clear, that as an institution, the Ombudsman for Children needed to build their trust. Forced migration can have the effect of making it difficult for asylum seekers and refugees to develop trusting relationships, and research with separated children living in Ireland had identified five specific causes of mistrust: past experiences; being accustomed to mistrust; being mistrusted by others; not knowing people well; and concerns about truth-telling (Ní Raghallaigh, 2014, p. 82). Their experiences prior to arrival in Ireland interacted with the challenges of integration and of an uncertain future, including the fear of being deported, and taken together, these factors created a situation where 'trusting became a huge challenge' (Ní Raghallaigh, 2014, p. 96). In this regard, the two young people from the Youth Advisory Panel were key to building bridges as they helped to establish trust between the separated children and Ombudsman for Children staff. The young advisors subsequently took on active roles as members of the project team, working alongside the Ombudsman's team in the project (Charles, 2009).

The planning of the project involved a series of preparatory meetings and discussions with key organisations and agencies working with separated children (Charles, 2009, p. 21). In contrast to the project on children in prison, in Chapter 7, the relevant authorities (the HSE) were instrumental in facilitating the roll out of the project, co-ordinating communication with all hostels and residential centres and requesting their co-operation in advance of engagement by the Ombudsman for Children. Crucially, their support for the project continued throughout the nine months (Charles, 2009, p. 21).

The Ombudsman's team visited nine of the ten accommodation centres in which separated children lived in order to make initial contact with the children and the staff and to invite the children to an open day, to be held in the offices of the Ombudsman (Charles, 2009). The Ombudsman's experience had indicated that a personalised invitation would be more likely to encourage the children to attend and as a result, personalised cards were issued to each young person inviting them to the office for the open day (Charles, 2009). Invitations were also issued to staff, key workers and social workers. In total, 48 children and young people came to the open day (Charles, 2009). The two young people from the Ombudsman for Children's youth advisory panel, Leylah and Ahmed, opened the day by introducing the Ombudsman for Children and their work and this peer-led approach was instrumental in building trust and relationships between the institution and the young people (Charles,

2009, p. 24). It also assisted the children and young people's understanding of the office as a unique body, independent of Government (Charles, 2009, p. 24). Over the course of several summer months, there were 22 group meetings with what became the advisory group and an additional number of young people who turned up for a 'drop-in time' option (Charles, 2009, p. 24). The 'drop-in time' was established for young people who wished to discuss their experience or raise an issue on a one-to-one basis (Charles, 2009, p. 27). The series of engagements sought to explore with the children what the key issues were in their lives from a children's rights perspective, and together with input from representatives and stakeholders provided the substantial basis for the case for reform.

## 8.4 Building the Case for Reform

Drawing on the consultation with separated children and with advocacy strengthened by their experiences, the Ombudsman for Children published its report on the key concerns and recommendations that required Government attention (Charles, 2009).

### *8.4.1 Legislative Reform*

At the time, the Immigration, Residence and Protection legislation was making its way through Oireachtas (Parliament) and the Ombudsman for Children was invited to make observations on the Bill. Based on the consultation with the separated children, the Ombudsman for Children (2008, p. 5) advised that in consideration of the legislation, the following CRC provisions should govern law and policy in this area, namely.

- the right to non-discrimination;
- the right for a child's best interests to be a primary consideration in matters which affect the child;
- the right to family or appropriate care and;
- the right for a child to be heard in all matters affecting him or her, with his or her views being given due weight in accordance with the child's age and maturity.

While noting some positive aspects, the Ombudsman submitted that the principal concern with the Bill was that it did not sufficiently take account of the particular vulnerability of children and the need to provide them with special assistance and protection. Highlighting that separated children face seeking international protection particular barriers realising their rights, the Ombudsman recommended that a general provision be included in the Bill to require that 'children's best interests shall be a primary consideration at all times and in all decisions affecting them' (OCO, 2008, p. 5).

### *8.4.2 Article 2 Non-Discrimination*

It was evident from the Separated Children Project that these children received a lower standard of care than children in the mainstream care system (Charles, 2009) and this was highlighted as a serious concern. They were mainly accommodated in non-registered 'hostel' centres, not subject to inspection or oversight (Charles, 2009, p. 22), in clear breach of obligations under Article 2 of the CRC. The Ombudsman for Children recommended that this practice should cease (Charles, 2009, p. 53).

### *8.4.3 Asylum Process*

The young people consulted by the Ombudsman for Children described the asylum process as very stressful, not child friendly and not sensitive to their unique situation (Charles, 2009, p. 30). They reported that recounting their experiences was 'very daunting and emotional' and recommended that the best way to support them through the process was to have a 'supportive and empathetic interviewer' who listened (Charles, 2009, p. 30). They described official correspondence about their status as 'scary and unfriendly' (Charles, 2009, p. 31), with one young person producing his correspondence with the salutation 'Dear. Mr. Child' (Charles, 2009, p. 38).

### *8.4.4* **Education**

Education was identified as a high priority for the majority of separated children consulted by the Ombudsman (Charles, 2009, p. 44). They described the positive difference that supportive and encouraging teachers could have (Charles, 2009, p. 54) but expressed considerable frustration at the inability to access further or higher education (Charles, 2009, p. 25) due to its prohibitive cost (Charles, 2009; McGuire & Pollak, 2016). There has been much public goodwill towards children and young people in the asylum system in Ireland, with donations through philanthropic grants and non-governmental organisations (McGuire & Pollak, 2016). Some third level institutions have also introduced a scholarship programme for young people in the asylum system (McGuire & Pollak, 2016) and there is now a government scheme in this area (Department of Further and Higher Education, Research, Innovation and Science, 2020). An additional concern for the small number of girls who were mothers was the requirement for them to pay a percentage of the childcare costs if they wanted to return to full-time education. The cost was prohibitive to the extent that this policy effectively precluded girls with a child from returning to school (Charles, 2009).

### 8.4.5 *Absence of an Independent Guardian/Adviser*

Good practice recommends that an independent guardian or adviser be appointed as soon as a separated child is identified, in order to advise and support children through the process (Separated Children in Europe Programme, 2004, p. 16). In Ireland, at the time, children did not have access to an independent guardian/adviser, meaning that the separated children frequently had to navigate administrative and other processes alone (Charles, 2009). In a more extreme situation, a child who went missing had no advocate to ensure everything is done to trace them.

### 8.4.6 *Complaints Mechanisms*

There was no effective internal mechanism for separated children to express concerns or complain about any aspect of their care. The hostels reported having 'complaints boxes', which most children reported being unaware of, or for the few that were aware, cited their positioning beside the reception and lack of anonymity as a barrier to their use (Charles, 2009, p. 40). While most children reported feeling too intimidated to speak out, when they did complain, others reported that their complaints were not always dealt with properly or in a respectful manner (Charles, 2009).

### 8.4.7 *Aftercare and Protection*

Ireland's approach to aftercare for separated children who reach the age of 18 is recognised to be 'problematic' (Ní Raghallaigh & Thornton, 2017, p. 386). The migrant status of aged-out children takes precedence over their departure from state care, which means that on reaching 18 years, they are placed in direct provision, the system of bed, board and weekly monetary payments, as opposed to being treated as children emerging from care in need of aftercare support (Ní Raghallaigh & Thornton, 2017). At the time of the Ombudsman's consultation, there was in place a policy of dispersing young people once they had reached the age of 18 years, without any aftercare provision or support (Charles, 2009, p. 54). At the time of the consultation, the HSE was in the process of developing a national intercultural health strategy (HSE, 2008b) which recognised separated children as a very vulnerable group, requiring responsive and coordinated interventions (HSE, 2008b). Nonetheless, there were serious concerns about young people at risk, with anecdotal accounts of sexual exploitation in the form of prostitution and accounts of child trafficking (HSE, 2008b).

### 8.4.8 *Out of Hours Support*

There was significant concern about children at risk having no supervision in the hostels after 5 pm in the evening. This heightened the risks faced by the separated children impacted, including from trafficking or other harm (Charles, 2009, p. 54).

## 8.5 Creative Approaches to Chronicling the Children's Experience

Over the course of the Ombudsman's nine-month project consulting with separated children, in addition to sharing their experiences of living in the hostels, young people were involved in three main activities set out here.

### 8.5.1 *Dublin—Your City, Our City*

In the course of early conversation, the children and young people decided they wanted to create something for other separated children arriving in Ireland in the future (OCO, 2009a). They came up with the idea of a guidebook that would include some key practical information about life in Ireland, to help young people adjust to their new life (Charles, 2009). Sessions on the guidebook were facilitated by the liaison officers, who had lived experience of being a separated child (Charles, 2009). The young people identified seven key areas where young people would benefit from more practical information: education; health and well-being; transport; leisure and hangouts; religion and spirituality; support groups; and service providers (OCO, 2009a). Along with the two publications, the guidebook was published with photographs of the young people's artwork undertaken during their summer holidays.

### 8.5.2 *'All I Have to Say'*

This next publication was a series of 'stories' about young people's lived experience prior to their arrival in Ireland (OCO, 2009b). The idea emerged from the young people's desire to create a better understanding of who separated children are and their experiences in their home countries (Charles, 2009, p. 27). The purpose of this work was to help raise awareness about separated children because little was known about them, they were not in the public consciousness and as a result, not high on the political agenda (OCO, 2009b, p. 9). As with all of the work, engagement in the story telling was entirely optional. The young people had linguistic and emotional support, could recount in their preferred language and also had the assistance of a creative writer to offer guidance as appropriate (Charles, 2009, p. 27). Thirteen children and young people chose to participate. They all reported that they found it emotionally difficult but wanted to do it.

### 8.5.3 *Creative Art and Photography*

The Ombudsman for Children partnered with an art gallery, the Hugh Lane Gallery in Dublin, for this part of the project (Charles, 2009). The children and young people worked with an artist to take photographs, produce models on their ideas of how the capital city might look if they were in charge and other artwork that captured their key messages. There was no problem recruiting young people for this aspect of the work, with all of the young people involved in the project reporting how much they enjoyed this aspect of the project. This artwork was used in all of the three publications for this project, in addition to being exhibited in the Hugh Lane Gallery (Charles, 2009).

## 8.6 Conclusion

This chapter outlined a case study of engaging with an especially vulnerable group of children about their treatment and their rights. With a methodology informed by the duty on the Ombudsman for Children to ensure children's voices are heard and their rights promoted, each element of the Separated Children Project sought to support them in documenting their experiences, with a view to promoting reform in law and policy while also supporting the children themselves to raise awareness about their circumstances in a creative and peer-led manner.

The project originated in multiple meetings with officials from the two government departments responsible for separated children from their port of entry to their care in state-run institutions, and culminated in a published report, 'Separated children living in Ireland', which brought about change on a number of levels. First, by July 2011, the HSE reported that the practice of placing separated children seeking asylum in hostels had ended (HSE, 2011). Second, the Children and Family Services began to implement an 'Equity of Care Policy' to ensure that all children and young people receive the same level of care as that afforded to indigenous children (HSE, 2011). In the Greater Dublin area, a specialist Separated Children Seeking Asylum (SCSA) social work team was established, consisting of four residential assessment units in Dublin that are registered children's homes. On arrival, children receive a multidisciplinary assessment, with medical, educational and social work components, and their care placement, usually in foster care, depends on their assessed needs (HSE, 2011, p. 79). The SCSA social work team operates a 'reunification service whereby immigration authorities refer families or adults presenting with children in cases where parentage or guardianship is not apparent' (HSE, 2011, p. 79). There is also an aftercare service in certain circumstances (HSE, 2011, p. 79).

The Ombudsman for Children's engagement with separated children was thus successful in bringing about substantial change, ensuring that the children's experiences of their rights informed the reform of law, policy and services that impact on these children. Deprived of more robust legal powers to challenge the treatment of these children, this multi-dimensional and creative project worked instead to give visibility and voice to a highly marginalised group of children, in a way that built a connection between them and the Ombudsman for Children. Despite their vulnerability, the Ombudsman's project was an important reminder of the resilience and the capacity of children to have their voices heard and to advocate for better rights protections—for themselves and others—notwithstanding the precariousness of their own status. That is not to say that the children and young people who participated in this project had not experienced trauma and many indeed had residual and ongoing emotional challenges. However, the project was an important reminder for the Ombudsman for Children that vulnerability, resilience and agency can and do co-exist in children's lives. The nature of the project—including its peer-led advocacy as an early example of children as human rights defenders—also affirmed the children and young people's desire to be viewed as 'active survivors' rather than 'passive victims'. In this respect, the engagement process—perhaps because and not despite the absence of the Ombudsman's power to investigate—became a more powerful use of advocacy, awareness raising and capacity building than might otherwise have been the case. The fact that this was true for the Ombudsman's office, as well as for policymakers whose actions it influenced, makes it all the more important.

## References

Arnold, S., Ryan, C., & Quinn, E. (2018). *Ireland's response to recent trends in international protection applications* (ESRI Research Series, No. 72).

Charles, K. (2009). *Separated children living in Ireland: A report by the Ombudsman for Children's Office*. Ombudsman for Children's Office.

Crowley, U., Gilmartin, M., & Kitchin, R. (2008). Race and immigration in contemporary Ireland. In *New geographies of race and racism* (pp. 141–156). Ashgate Publishing.

Department of Further and Higher Education, Research, Innovation and Science. (2020). *Minister Harris announces changes to the student support scheme for people living in Direct Provision*. Press Release. Available at: https://www.gov.ie/en/press-release/4c832-minister-harris-announces-changes-to-the-student-support-scheme-for-people-living-in-direct-provision/. Accessed 11 Apr 2021.

Health Service Executive. (2008a). *Review of adequacy of services for children and families*. Available at: https://www.hse.ie/eng/services/publications/children/reviewofadequacy.html. Accessed 6 Apr 2021.

Health Service Executive. (2008b). *National intercultural health strategy 2007–2012*.

Health Service Executive. (2011). *Review of adequacy for HSE children and family services*. Available at: https://www.hse.ie/eng/services/publications/children/reviewofadequacy2011.pdf. Accessed 6 Apr 2021.
Keogh, A. F., & Whyte, J. (2003). *Getting on: The experiences and aspirations of immigrant students in second level schools linked to the Trinity Access Programmes*. Children's Research Centre, Trinity College Dublin.
Kilkelly, U. (2007). *Barriers to the realisation of children's rights in Ireland*. Ombudsman for Children's Office.
McGuire, P., & Pollak, S. (2016, October 25). No asylum in Ireland's education system. *The Irish Times*. Available at: https://www.irishtimes.com/news/education/no-asylum-in-ireland-s-education-system-1.2834317. Accessed 6 Apr 2021.
Ní Raghallaigh, M. (2014). The causes of mistrust amongst asylum seekers and refugees: Insights from research with unaccompanied asylum-seeking minors living in the Republic of Ireland. *Journal of Refugee Studies, 27*(1), 82–100.
Ní Raghallaigh, M., & Gilligan, R. (2010). Active survival in the lives of unaccompanied minors: Coping strategies, resilience, and the relevance of religion. *Child & Family Social Work, 15*(2), 226–237.
Ní Raghallaigh, M., & Thornton, L. (2017). Vulnerable childhood, vulnerable adulthood: Direct provision as aftercare for aged-out separated children seeking asylum in Ireland. *Critical Social Policy, 37*(3), 386–404.
O'Brien, C. (2007, July 3). Failings of hostels for trafficked children raised. *The Irish Times*. Available at: https://www.irishtimes.com/news/failings-of-hostels-for-trafficked-children-raised-1.948007. Accessed 6 Apr 2021.
Ombudsman for Children Act. (2002).
Ombudsman for Children. (2005). *Annual report 2005*. Ombudsman for Children's Office.
Ombudsman for Children. (2006a). *Report of the Ombudsman for Children to the UN Committee on the Rights of the Child on the occasion of the examination of Ireland's second report to the committee*. Ombudsman for Children's Office. Available at: https://www.oco.ie/app/uploads/2006/04/ReportonexaminationofirelandssecondreportApril20061.pdf. Accessed 6 Apr 2021.
Ombudsman for Children. (2006b). *Respecting children: Annual report of the Ombudsman for Children's Office April 2005-December 2006*. Ombudsman for Children's Office.
Ombudsman for Children. (2008). *Advice of the Ombudsman for Children on the Immigration, Residence and Protection Bill 2008*. Ombudsman for Children's Office. Available at: https://www.oco.ie/app/uploads/2008/08/AdviceonimmigrationresidenceandprotectionMarch2008.pdf. Accessed 6 Apr 2021.
Ombudsman for Children. (2009a). *Dublin—Your city, our city*. A guide compiled by separated children. Ombudsman for Children's Office. Available

at: https://www.oco.ie/childrens-rights/consulting-with-young-people/past-projects/separated-children-2009/. Accessed 12 Apr 2021.

Ombudsman for Children. (2009b). *'All I have to say', separated children in their own words*. Ombudsman for Children's Office. Available at: https://www.oco.ie/childrens-rights/consulting-with-young-people/past-projects/separated-children-2009/. Accessed 12 Apr 2021.

Ruhs, M., & Quinn, E. (2009). *Ireland: From rapid immigration to recession* [online]. Migration Policy Institute Paper, Washington. Available at: https://www.migrationpolicy.org/article/ireland-rapid-immigration-recession. Accessed 6 Apr 2021.

Separated Children in Europe Programme. (2004). *Statement of good practice* (3rd ed.). Save the Children & UNHCR.

The Irish Times. (2006, April 17). UN members to see how Irish children are treated. *The Irish Times*. Available at: https://www.irishtimes.com/news/un-members-to-see-how-irish-children-are-treated-1.779464. Accessed 6 Apr 2021.

UN Committee on the Rights of the Child. (1998, February 4). *Concluding observations: Ireland*. CRC/C/15/Add.85.

UN Committee on the Rights of the Child. (2002, November 15). *General Comment No. 2 (2002): The role of independent national human rights institutions in the promotion and protection of the rights of the child*. CRC/GC/2002/2.

UN Committee on the Rights of the Child. (2005, September 1). *General Comment No. 6 (2005): Treatment of unaccompanied and separated children outside their country of origin*. CRC/GC/2005/6.

UN Committee on the Rights of the Child. (2006, September 29). *Concluding observations: Ireland*. CRC/C/IRL/CO/2.

UN Convention on the Rights of the Child (CRC). (1989).

UNHCR, the UN Refugee Agency. (2018). *Global trends: Forced displacement in 2018*. Available at: https://www.unhcr.org/globaltrends2018/. Accessed 6 Apr 2021.

UNHCR, the UN Refugee Agency. (2019). *Global trends: Forced displacement in 2019*. Available at: https://www.unhcr.org/globaltrends2019/. Accessed 6 Apr 2021.

CHAPTER 9

# Conclusions

**Abstract** This book sought to consider the experience of the Irish Ombudsman for Children as an example of how a national human rights institution for children can meet international standards. A clear statutory mandate, and creative and integrated use of powers, have all helped to ensure that the potential of the institution to reform law, policy and practice relating to children's rights is maximised. Lessons can be learned from the first ten years of this new office, established in 2004, as to how legislative power can be translated into strategic action. Experiences indicate that what is instrumental is how the institution's powers are used as much as what they are used to achieve.

**Keywords** Ombudsman for Children · International standards · Reform · Soft power · Legislative powers · Strategic action · Mandate

## 9.1 Introduction

The adoption of the Convention on the Rights of the Child in 1989 has led to a growth in the interest in National Human Rights Institutions (NHRIs) for children around the world. The diversity in the institutions established at local, regional and national level is remarkable and reflected



U. Kilkelly and E. Logan, *National Independent Human Rights Institutions for Children*,
https://doi.org/10.1007/978-3-030-80275-2_9

by a similar diversity in the countries and regions that they serve. This book set out to document the lessons to be learned from over a decade of children's rights advocacy, reform and monitoring with a national human rights institution for children that has become a model of its kind. Set against the expectations of international standards including the Paris Principles and the Committee on the Rights of the Child's General Comment No. 2, the book explained the origins of the Irish Ombudsman for Children, outlined the legislative model that underpins the institution and identified some of the different ways in which its mandate was used to promote and protect children's rights in Ireland. The approach was more selective than comprehensive, with a focus on sharing from practice the creative and diverse ways in which legislative power can translate into strategic action on children's rights. Each chapter provided examples of how the functions of the Ombudsman for Children—to raise awareness about children's rights, offer guidance to Government and investigate complaints—have been used. The case studies—on the rights of children in prison and separated children seeking international protection—demonstrated how the views and experiences of children themselves can help to bring about change in even the most difficult areas. The aim of this final chapter therefore is to draw some conclusions from the Irish experience for an international audience of what was most important in achieving successful reform. These are divided into three sections: first, the origins of the institution and the importance of the legislation; second, the exercise of the institution's powers and third, the chapter concludes with some recommendations for the future.

## 9.2 Origins of the Institution and the Legislation

As with many national human rights institutions for children, the Irish Ombudsman for Children was established against a backdrop of child abuse and ill-treatment. While the events outlined in Chapter 2 presented Ireland's 'watershed' moment, it was important that this opportunity was seized by the children's rights community to influence the Government's response. In Ireland's case, the leadership of the Children's Rights Alliance, a non-governmental organisation set up after Ireland's ratification of the Convention on the Rights of the Child, was key in supporting a process that ultimately gathered cross-sectoral support for the new institution. The initiative of the Alliance, in supporting a process of research and consultation around the most appropriate model of children's rights institution for Ireland, was both timely and influential in garnering political consensus around the model. Early in Ireland's engagement in this process, the role of the UN standards was key and members of the international community were also influential in securing consensus around the form that the proposed institution was to take. The fact that early children's rights institutions, like that in Norway, were set up as an ombudsman probably guided Ireland in that direction. However, it was important too that Ireland had experience of the ombudsman model in that what was familiar was less likely to be feared. National context proved vital.

The international standards on NHRIs, set out in Chapter 2, provided important guidance for the development of the Ombudsman for Children. Its establishment as an independent institution has been fundamentally important to the development of the office and has helped to protect it from political influence. Its independence has also strengthened its integrity enabling the Ombudsman to speak out on sensitive, controversial and difficult issues. It has also meant that interventions—like consulting with children in prison to bring about reform as explained in Chapter 7—could be undertaken without fear of reprisal.

The different powers set out in the legislation have given the Ombudsman a range of options that can be adapted and applied, with creativity to confront different children's right issues They range of powers have allowed the institution to flex the approach required, depending on the matter concerned, combining powers and functions as appropriate. This is neatly demonstrated by the Separated Children Project set out in Chapter 8, but it is also clear from various examples that innovation and a child-centred approach have helped to maximise the power for reform. In this regard, the rights basis of the legislation has proven to be critically important to the approach taken and the duty of the Ombudsman to protect and promote children's rights has ensured that the institution has the breadth of mandate to address a diverse range of issues that impact and affect the rights and lives of children. The explicit reference in the legislation to the Convention on the Rights of the Child has helped to strengthen this approach further.

While it is regrettable that the Ombudsman for Children does not have constitutional standing, the legislative basis of the institution has helped to protect it from political influence and public pressure. While the slow pace of parliamentary reform in Ireland can be criticised for other reasons, it does have the advantage that knee-jerk or quick-fix legislative proposals are difficult to implement. Proposals to subsume the Ombudsman for Children into other bodies or to amend the mandate of the office have so far been difficult to achieve. The integrity of the office and strong stakeholder relationships, built up over many years, have also helped the institution to withstand this kind of pressure.

## 9.3 Exercising the Ombudsman's Powers

As the book illustrates, the Ombudsman for Children has multiple distinct powers—to raise awareness about children's rights, to offer guidance and advice to Government on legislation and to investigate complaints received by the office for example. As the book also demonstrates these can be exercised in a discrete manner, in isolation, but they can also be used in an integrated manner with multiple functions deployed simultaneously. For instance, as Chapter 4 shows, the combination of research, consultation and awareness raising helped to promote children's rights through the 'Big Ballot' project, establishing the credibility of the Ombudsman in the very early days of its establishment. Alternatively, as Chapters 7 and 8 explain, consultation with children in prison and with separated children in the asylum system, helped to compensate for the absence of the Ombudsman's investigations function in these areas. Instead, it can be argued, the institution was forced to take a more ambitious and creative approach to reform, engaging directly with children themselves in overcoming institutional resistance to credibly 'speak truth to power'. Concerns that the Ombudsman for Children would be overwhelmed by the duty to investigate complaints have been overcome by taking a more systematic approach where possible, publishing special reports from time to time to draw attention to overarching and structural problems. Being proactive—at times setting the agenda—has proven to be as important as the duty to respond to the issues that are brought to the institution's attention. Given that the demands on a national institution will always exceed resources, being strategic and selective is vital to the effectiveness of the office.

The extent to which the institution evolved in line with children's rights principles has proven to be a hallmark of its approach and its credibility. The Ombudsman's connection to the children they serve is vital to every function and power of the office and the participation of children is perhaps the one area where ambition should never be limited by pragmatism.

## 9.4 Reviewing for the Future

The story of the Ombudsman for Children demonstrates the importance of a strong legislative basis, important personal leadership and vision and an approach informed by credibility, integrity and authority. While some of the deficits of the legislation were highlighted early on and advocacy brought about their remedy, this is not the case universally. A significant gap in the Ombudsman for Children Act 2002 remains the absence of legal powers. The institution cannot initiate legal action on behalf of children. Nor can it intervene as an amicus curiae or friend of the court even though that power is enjoyed by the Irish Human Rights and Equality Commission. This inequity between institutions should be remedied. The remit of the institution to cover areas previously excluded or to clarify its existing mandate in relation to children in police custody and in the asylum system, for instance, should be addressed without delay. Consideration should also be given to enabling the institution to monitor and inspect residential and other institutions and to cross-refer from other bodies where its expertise allows. Extension of the mandate of the Ombudsman complaint function to include private bodies and institutions should be given careful consideration in light of the extent to which children's lives are now impacted by corporate and commercial entities, especially in the digital space.

While this book has focused largely on initiatives and interventions that have enjoyed success of one kind or another, there are some areas where closer scrutiny is required. For instance, little is known about the institution's effectiveness in influencing legislation as to date no audit of this function has been undertaken. Scrutiny of the complaint function is also recommended so that the use of this power can be better understood. Overall, there is a need for greater scrutiny in the functioning of the office, including by the Oireachtas (Parliament) to which and a research and evaluation agenda would be both timely and complementary in supporting the institution to ensure its powers and resources are used to maximum strategic effect.

In summary, it is clear that the Ombudsman for Children has made its mark since its arrival into Ireland's children's rights community and its success can be attributed to many factors—a strong legislative footing with a broad children's rights-based mandate, a supportive stakeholder community that had campaigned for its establishment and willed it to succeed and the awful legacy of child abuse that meant a weak or disabled institution would not be tolerated. Important too has been the appointment into the office of strong leadership and creative and talented staff with the ambition and drive to make a difference in children's lives. Of course, it is difficult to say whether children's lives are better now than in 2004 when the Ombudsman for Children was first appointed. Objectively, however, children are no longer detained in prison, separated children are in family care rather than residential centres and the area of child protection is now the responsibility of a dedicated statutory agency. Thousands of children have had their complaints resolved. The Ombudsman for Children did not achieve these reforms alone, but together with stakeholders, decision-makers and children and their families who desired change. However, the Ombudsman did succeed in harmonising and at times amplifying these voices to advocate and press for change in the treatment of children. And the office has continued to develop and grow, along with the children it has served. This, at the very least, was where success was truly achieved.

# Index

A
Academia, 8, 80
Accountability, 35, 67, 68, 77
Adoption, 4, 14, 16, 19, 46, 48, 59, 72, 75, 139
Advice, 2, 32, 55, 66, 67, 69, 71–74, 76–78, 81, 108, 142
Advocacy, 9, 19–24, 26, 30, 31, 34, 36, 38, 53, 54, 78, 88, 129, 135, 143
Africa, 4, 6
After-care supports, 97
Age and maturity, 94
Amicus briefs, 40
Annual Report, 35, 49, 51, 67–70, 77, 88, 91–93, 100, 106, 107
Asia, 4, 6
Asylum, 39, 49, 53, 71, 76, 95, 124–126, 128, 130, 131, 134, 142, 143
Australia, 6
Awareness
raising, 2, 20, 23, 30, 32, 36, 37, 49, 58, 60, 90, 142

B
Barriers, 8, 22–24, 52–54, 68, 69, 94, 104, 106, 114, 130
Best interests of the child, 4, 35, 37, 79, 80, 87, 89, 93
Bullying, 49, 91, 95, 107, 114

C
Canada, 6
Child abuse, 30, 32, 34, 40, 140, 144
Child death review, 73, 74
Children Act, 2001, 105
Children's Rights Alliance, 30, 31, 40, 140
Children's rights, education, 5, 30, 32, 50, 51
Children's rights, participation, 17, 25, 26, 46, 49, 53, 54, 57, 59, 60, 66, 94


U. Kilkelly and E. Logan, *National Independent Human Rights Institutions for Children*,
https://doi.org/10.1007/978-3-030-80275-2

Children's rights, promotion, 3–5, 7, 8, 14, 17, 18, 23, 25, 32, 34, 35, 37, 47, 67
Children's rights, protection, 3, 5, 8, 14, 17, 18, 23, 25, 37, 67, 72, 79, 81, 99
Civil partnership, 72
Civil society, 8, 9, 18, 23, 30, 36, 40, 58, 77, 80, 119
Comhairle na nÓg (youth councils), 50
Commissioner for children, Commissioners, 59, 74
Commission to Inquire into Child Abuse, 31
Committee for the Prevention of Torture (CPT), 71, 117
Committee on the Rights of the Child, CRC Committee, 2, 3, 14, 16, 30, 33, 37, 46, 52, 66, 86, 117, 124
Communication, 17, 47, 90, 93, 97, 98, 110, 114, 127, 128
Complaints
  handling, 37, 39, 86, 89, 91, 93
Concluding Observations, CRC Committee, 33, 126
Confidentiality, 108
Constitutional referendum, 75
Consultation, children, 26, 34, 46, 49, 53, 55, 56, 58, 75, 129
Convention on the Rights of the Child (CRC)
  Article 2, 4, 17, 130, 125–127
  Article 3, 4
  Article 4, 2, 14
  Article 12, 4, 17, 48, 127
  Article 19, 114
  Article 24, 73, 112
  Article 37, 113
Council of Europe
  Commissioner for Human Rights, 70, 117
  Convention on Action Against Trafficking in Human Beings, 74
  Guidelines on Child-friendly Healthcare, 73
Court proceedings, 74

## D

Dáil na bPáistí (children's parliament), 50
Dáil na nÓg (youth parliament), 50
Defence Forces, 39
Delays, 31, 90, 94–96, 115, 143
Department, of
  Children, 46, 59, 105
  Education, 91, 92, 105
  Justice, 73, 105
Detention, 38, 74, 76, 104, 105, 107–109, 111, 115, 117–119, 127
Digital consent, 75
Direct Provision, 39, 49, 132
Disability, 93

## E

Education, 5, 15, 27, 30, 32, 47, 50–57, 68, 69, 73, 77, 79, 81, 91, 92, 95, 98, 104–107, 112, 113, 124, 130, 131, 133
Enforcement, 15, 21, 22
European Network of Ombudspersons for Children (ENOC), 5, 8, 20, 70
European Rules for Juveniles subject to Sanctions and Measures, 109

**F**
Family, 33, 34, 52, 54, 56, 57, 71, 74, 76, 77, 80, 81, 95, 113, 114, 124, 126, 129, 134
Foster care, 92, 134

**G**
General Comments, CRC Committee, 2, 3, 7, 14, 16–18, 26, 46, 127
  No. 2, 2, 4, 6, 7, 9, 18, 30, 37, 47, 48, 69, 86, 127, 140
  No. 5, 46
Girls, 131
Global Alliance of NHRIs, 4

**H**
Harmonisation, 3, 17, 20, 66, 68, 72, 75, 82
Havana Rules, Juveniles Deprived of Liberty, 109
Health, rights, 7, 52, 54, 57, 69, 73, 79, 95, 112, 133
Housing, rights, 7, 92, 95, 97
Human rights, education, 15, 47, 50, 51, 58

**I**
Impact assessment, children's rights, 77, 82
Independence, 3, 5–7, 15, 17, 20, 21, 23–26, 35, 37, 38, 48, 75, 81, 89, 100, 104, 141
Information, 3, 15, 23, 25, 40, 51–53, 60, 68, 70, 87, 89, 90, 93–96, 110, 133
Inquiry, 7, 31, 88
Inspection, 104, 107, 114, 116, 130
Inspector of Prisons, 38, 106, 107, 110, 115, 116
Inter-agency working, 97
International, 2, 3, 6, 7, 9, 10, 14–16, 18, 19, 23, 25–27, 30–34, 37, 40, 46, 50, 58, 67, 69–71, 73–75, 86, 88, 93, 98, 104, 108, 109, 111, 112, 117, 119, 124, 125, 140, 141
Investigation, 7, 10, 16, 17, 19–21, 26, 30, 32, 35–38, 40, 48, 73, 86–92, 96, 97, 99, 100, 106, 107, 120, 142
Irish Human Rights and Equality Commission, 37, 143

**K**
Kilkenny Incest Investigation, 31

**L**
Latin America, 6
Legislation, 2, 3, 6, 19, 30–37, 39, 40, 47, 49, 66–69, 71, 72, 74–76, 78, 81, 86, 87, 89, 99, 104, 106, 118, 129
  monitoring, 5, 6, 19, 33, 68, 94, 104, 117
  reform, 71, 129

**M**
Maladministration, 6, 99
Mandate, 2, 7, 15, 16, 18–22, 24–26, 34, 37, 40, 48, 66–69, 72, 82, 86, 99, 100, 104, 117–119, 127, 140–144
Media, 15, 31, 47, 48, 55, 58, 109
  multi-media resources, 56, 90
Mental health services, 73, 96, 107

**N**
National human rights institutions (NHRIs), 3, 4, 6, 14–27, 37, 46, 59, 66, 127, 141

Networking, 70
Non-disclosure of criminal records, 72
Non-governmental organisations (NGO), 31, 131, 140
Norway, 5, 18, 24, 31, 32, 141

**O**
Oberstown Children Detention Campus, 105, 119
Oireachtas (Parliament), 7, 32, 35–37, 40
Ombudsman for Children, 2, 5–10, 19, 20, 27, 30–40, 46–51, 53–59, 67–77, 80–82, 86–91, 95–100, 104, 106–109, 115–119, 124–130, 133, 134, 140–144
Ombudsman for Children Act 2002, 6, 30, 34, 36, 40, 52, 67, 70, 71, 87, 88, 99, 104, 107, 118, 127, 143
Ombudsman for Children Bill, 34, 38
Optional Protocol on the Sale of Children, Child Prostitution and Pornography, CRC, 16, 74

**P**
Parents, 22, 48, 55, 56, 79, 95, 126
Paris Principles, 3, 4, 6, 9, 14–16, 18, 20, 21, 23, 26, 30, 36–38, 66, 86, 140
Parliamentary committee, 67, 74, 78, 79
Parliamentary debate, 31, 32, 76
Participation, children in decision-making, 46
Participation lab, 50
Peer-led, 128, 134, 135
Play and Recreation, 53, 57
Police, Gardaí, 38, 39, 116
Political consensus, 31, 74, 141
Poverty, 53, 125
Power, soft, 5, 7, 9, 46, 59, 104, 119
Power, to investigate, 9, 21, 36, 118, 135
Prison, 10, 38, 104–108, 111–117, 119, 128, 140–142, 144
Public body, 87, 88, 90, 95–97, 99, 100
Public engagement, 5, 68
Public interest, 91

**R**
Ratification, 5, 15, 31, 50, 140
Refugee children, 124, 125
Remedies, 5, 21, 22, 27, 33, 56, 88
Research, 5, 7, 21, 30, 32, 34, 35, 37, 47, 52–55, 58, 60, 69, 73, 93, 98, 104, 106, 124, 127, 128, 131, 140, 142, 143
Resistance, 7, 8, 90, 100, 119, 142
Resources, 15, 18–20, 24, 25, 49, 55, 58, 59, 67, 68, 90, 96, 97, 99, 142, 143

**S**
School complaint procedures, 91
School curriculum, 55
Schools, 7, 50, 51, 54–57, 59, 91, 95, 104, 105, 119
Secondary victimisation, 72
Separated children, 10, 76, 124–134, 140, 142, 144
Sexual exploitation, 71, 132
Sexual offences, 72, 74, 77, 79
Social media, 51, 59, 60
Social welfare, 95
Special reports, 92, 100, 142
Stakeholders, 54, 57, 58, 74, 108, 129, 142, 144
St Patrick's Institution, 104–108, 119
Strategic action, 36, 50
Sustainable Development Goals, 4

Sweden, 19, 24, 31, 32
Systemic rights violations, 22

**T**
Teachers, 50, 54, 55, 57, 58, 114, 130
Thematic reviews of complaints, 92
Trafficking, 72–75, 125, 132
Trauma, 135
Traveller children, 53

**U**
UN Committee against Torture (CAT), 71, 117, 118
UN High Commissioner on Refugees, 70
UNICEF, 2, 5, 14, 20, 22, 25, 48
United Nations Convention on the Rights of the Child (CRC), 30, 124
Universal Periodic Review, 71
UN Palermo Protocol on Trafficking, 74
UN Special Rapporteur on the sale and sexual exploitation of children, 71
UN Special Representative on Violence against Children, 70

**V**
Vienna Declaration, 14, 15
Visiting Committee, 106, 107, 115
Vote, 52, 54–57

**W**
Watchdog, 76
Website, 51, 57

**Y**
Youth Advisory Panel, 49, 55, 127, 128
Youth justice, 52, 71, 105
Youth projects, 51

The manufacturer's authorised representative in the EU is Springer Nature Customer Service Centre GmbH, Europaplatz 3, 69115 Heidelberg, Germany. If you have any concerns regarding our products, please contact ProductSafety@springernature.com

Printed and bound by CPI Group (UK) Ltd, Croydon, CR0 4YY
30/09/2026
02225466-0015